PENGUIN BOO

On Yo

Short of cash? e time? Here are ... ideas for using your time and talent to earn the money to buy that longed-for hi-fi system, holiday or coat.

How about: asking local shops and tradespeople whether they need someone to add up their VAT and accounts, taking washing to the launderette, growing and selling herbs, restoring toys, cleaning the local zoo or even entering competitions? This book is bound to get you thinking, and earning! And you'll quite probably gain valuable experience of the world of work into the bargain.

There is also lots of helpful information about saving and investing your money, impressing your boss as a model employee, and, very importantly, staying within the laws governing your employment. Who knows, a spare-time job could turn out to be the foundation for the future.

Merry Archard was for thirteen years the family and home correspondent of the London *Evening Standard*. She is now a freelance writer.

+ Plus ▶

MERRY ARCHARD

On Your Bike!

Illustrated by David McKee

PENGUIN BOOKS

PENGUIN BOOKS

Published by the Penguin Group
27 Wrights Lane, London W8 5TZ, England
Viking Penguin Inc., 40 West 23rd Street, New York, New York 10010, USA
Penguin Books Australia Ltd, Ringwood, Victoria, Australia
Penguin Books Canada Ltd, 2801 John Street, Markham, Ontario, Canada L3R 1B4
Penguin Books (NZ) Ltd, 182–190 Wairau Road, Auckland 10, New Zealand

Penguin Books Ltd, Registered Offices: Harmondsworth, Middlesex, England

First published 1988

Made and printed in Great Britain by
Richard Clay Ltd, Bungay, Suffolk
Filmset in 10/11pt Univers Light

CONTENTS

1 INTRODUCTION

Want to earn some extra cash? Yearning for a bike, clothes, a guitar, a holiday, but your pocket-money won't stretch to it?

If you can't ask your parents for a loan or a pay increase, think of the fun and rewards of taking a spare-time job before you leave school.

Perhaps in this country we rely too much on Mum and Dad. In America, every boy and girl, poor or well-off, has an out-of-school job. They think it is an important part of growing up. So here are a few suggestions.

There are lots of possibilities for anybody willing, out of school hours, during weekends or holidays, and without taking adults' employment chances away from them. And you're bound to find something to suit you from the ideas inside, plus hints on how to get work (and keep it!), negotiate with your boss, and start feathering your own little money-nest.

Jobs you do for your own family, of course, are usually unpaid, unless your mother or father runs a business or farm. This is called family democracy or bartering (you help me and I'll help you)! But, much as you may enjoy your father giving you a slap on the back for cleaning the car till it sparkles, much as you may warm to Mum's smacking kiss for scrubbing out the oven, there is nothing like the real thrill of being independent, even if it's just in a small way, for the first time. (An hour a week is a start, isn't it?)

It's not ordinary pocket-money.
It's *your* money.
You are working for it.
Honestly.
With hard labour.

There is nothing in the world like that wonderful feeling of being able to stand on your own two feet for the first time, when you know you are free to spend the money you have earned on whatever or whomever you choose – yourself, a friend, your parents . . . Real freedom. At last!

Some parents automatically assume that, out of their loving clutches, you will spend your money on something silly or dangerous, like way-out, shoddy clothes, costly chocolates or comics for friends, a motorized

bike you are not ready to ride, or a dress you have not yet got the shape to wear. Perhaps, with the help of this book, you will be able to show them how you can raise the paper and coins to spend wisely – it could even be on something to surprise them!

Maybe the reason you would like to take a spare-time job is because you haven't the slightest idea what you want to do when you go out into the wide, wide earning world. School is a bit grey. Not one of the careers your teachers suggest seems to appeal. You feel a bit like your pet hamster in its cage, running round in circles, getting nowhere in exams. Everything seems boring. Well, you aren't a hamster, so cheer up and get going.

Drop negative, turn positive!

The famous painter Constable may have known what he wanted to do from the age of four, but then he was from a rich family. The equally famous painter Gauguin, who had very little money and had to take the first job he could find – as a clerk – didn't have the chance to make up his mind what he wanted to do until he was forty. Ex-Prime Minister Sir Harold Wilson chuckles at the picture of himself as an eight-year-old standing on the doorstep of No. 10 Downing Street. He hadn't an inkling that he would become the head of Britain's government forty years later.

Your parents and teachers are probably always on at you, asking you to tell them what you want to be when you grow up. It's all very well for them to talk, but how will you know if you haven't had a chance to try first?

Maybe you just aren't ready to make up your mind. You want to look around, think about things a while, try out a few different jobs over the holidays. Good for you! However disappointing a spare-time job may turn out to be, it will never be a dead loss.

True, some employers will nag worse than Mum; some throw scenes more than Dad; some jobs could turn out to be duller than Sunday afternoon television. But, when you've read the ideas and advice in this book, I hope you will discover that spare-time work can give you invaluable real-life experience – and lovely money, too!

2 ANYBODY CAN DO SOMETHING

Most people have some kind of special, individual talent. It is just a question of sitting down and pondering for a while, perhaps with one or two of your friends, about the kind of job you think you would enjoy doing and do better than most – the kind of work that may seem a miserable effort to some, but which you find rewarding and a pleasure.

Some young people have a way with babies. Your best friend might consider trying to bed down a restless two-year-old, while his parents are off to a party, boring and tiresome. You might consider it great fun romping round the nursery, reading fairy stories, having a nice kiss and cuddle before tucking in.

Some can't stand yappy dogs or miaowing cats. But you may have a special love of animals that makes looking after pets a delight – for you, the pets and your employers, who know they can happily leave them with you when they go away.

Lots of us take great satisfaction in housework, transforming a grubby, dusty chaos of a room into a clean and tidy lounge. For a householder who hates cleaning up, you would be a godsend.

Or maybe you like sorting out a jungle of a garden – seeing a pop star hair-style of a lawn transformed with a bit of clipping and mowing into a neat square of greensward, and choked seedlings and wilting bedding plants weeded, watered and staked so that a

wilderness of weeds becomes a flourishing riot of colour and scent.

Sometimes parents or friends may try to persuade you into taking a spare-time job that offers good money but not much interest for you. If you are desperate for cash, of course, you can stick it out in work you might consider a bit humdrum, not to say downright purgatory. Remember, though, that even the most menial, draggy, four-hours-every-Saturday stint can teach you a lot about how others have to live and, maybe, make you friends that could last a lifetime.

So what are your abilities (something, perhaps, your parents may not have appreciated)? As a start, to avoid finding yourself a square peg in a round hole, have a look at the Talent Chart below.

THE TALENT CHART

Tick your skills against this list, then turn to the jobs listed, detailed in Chapter 3:

Talent	Jobs
☐ **Artistic:** good at drawing, cartooning, handwriting, designing	A2, C8, D7, D8, L3, P7, P8, P10, R1, S1, T2
☐ **Tidy, Houseproud**	C1, C2, C4, H5, I3, J1, L1, P3, S8, U1, W1, W4
☐ **Love Babies**	B1, B2, B3, L6
☐ **Prefer Small Children**	B1, B3, B5, H3, L6, M1, P3
☐ **Fond of Animals and Pets**	C3, D4, D5, F3, P5, P6, S7, V2, Z1
☐ **Good with Old People**	F2, H4, M3, P4, W3
☐ **A Mind for Maths**	A1, C8, M3, S4
☐ **Outdoors Type**	A2, A3, B6, C7, D2, D3, D5, F1, F6, G2, G3, H1, H2, H3, I1, L2, L4, M3, M6, O1, P9, R3, S6, S7, S8, V1, W2, W3, W4, Y1
☐ **Sporting:** cycling, football, swimming, tennis, etc.	B5, C8, G3, Y1, Y2
☐ **Good at English, Reading**	B3, C8, L5
☐ **Diy Buff**	B4, D1, D7, F5, G1, J1, R1

☐ **Making and Mending Your Own Clothes**	C5, D6, D8, K1, M4
☐ **Bit of a Show-off, a Joker**	M1, M3, P3, S1, T1, T2, X1
☐ **Like Working with People**	A2, C6, H3, H4, H5, I1, L5, M1, M2, M3, M5, M6, P1, P3, R2, S3, S4, T2
☐ **Musical**	C8, G4, P3, S5, T1
☐ **Indoors Type**	C8, C9, F4, I2, T3

3 A–Z OF JOBS

(WHAT THEY INVOLVE AND HOW TO TACKLE THEM)

A1 ADDING UP ACCOUNTS AND VAT

If you are good at maths, there are plenty of small shopkeepers and one-person businesses such as tradesmen and tradeswomen without a head for figures who would gladly offer some of their profits to a young person who can do their adding, subtracting and computing for them. If your parents know anything about accountancy, so much the better, because you must be quite sure that your work is accurate. Make it clear to your employer that you are not a professional, but just doing the first, easy stages for him or her.

A2 ADVERTISING

To find a job dropping leaflets or advertising cards through letterboxes, look through the classified ads of your local newspaper. There are often a number of invitations for housewives or young people willing to earn money for a few hours by delivering material to houses. Or ring up any local business which you think might be on the look-out for more customers. Some might even ask you to deliver the leaflets or cards personally with a bit of sales talk. In this case, expect more pay – and be sure that you know the firm to be as honest, inexpensive and reliable as it says it is!

A3 APPLE-PICKING

You need not live in the country to earn money this way. Lots of elderly people in towns or cities have a few trees in their garden whose fruit they cannot pick themselves. So, if there are no commercial orchards near you, look around for over-fifties neighbours with some laden boughs.

A4 APPRENTICE . . .

. . . builder, plumber, decorator, garage mechanic, gardener, dressmaker, hairdresser, caterer, graphic designer (but not officially, of course) – almost any kind of job that interests you. If you want to do this for a living eventually, you will have to go through the proper training, but why not give yourself a head start – and decide whether it's really the career for you – by offering your services as a dogsbody?

Helping with pressing and hemming for the dress-maker round the corner, if you keep your eyes and ears open, will teach you a lot about cutting, fitting and fashion. It will also give you the kind of practical experience not usually offered at college if you decide on a design course.

Hauling the toolbag and holding the spanners and screwdrivers for a local electrician or plumber who needs a bit of extra help at rush times could save you a lot of homework if you choose to become one when you leave school and start your training proper. There are plenty of small set-ups who would be glad of a willing novice at holiday-time and who offer good pay.

And don't think of these jobs as sexist any more. Even if you're a girl with no ambitions to be an electrical engineer, you could still be welcome to a neighbour whose apprentice is off sick. You can console yourself not only with the money for a new dress, but with the knowledge that now you can mend the fuses and repair Mum's burnt-out iron plug! The same with plumbing – after a few sessions assisting with blocked drains and burst pipes you will never get in a panic when it happens in your house, because you will know where to turn off the stopcock and how to deal with blockages.

The same applies to boys in what used to be considered girls' jobs. After an Easter fortnight at a dress-maker's you will never have to plead with Mum or a girlfriend when you need your own clothes altered or repaired. In this way a fourteen-year-old I know is running up his own jackets and restyling his jeans to the envy of all his schoolmates – of both sexes!

B1 BABY-SITTING

This is the most popular gold-mine for would-be pocket-money earners. Only don't kill the goose that lays the golden egg (to mix a metaphor) by demanding too much money, or you won't be asked again. With regular baby-sitting you have a nice weekly 'wage' you can depend on, and your employers have the satisfaction of knowing they can rely on you.

When you offer to baby-sit for little ones you don't know, ask if you can come round one tea-time a couple of days beforehand to get to know them. Then they won't find you a frightening stranger, and will be much easier to amuse and bed down, or comfort if they wake when Mum and Dad are out. Ask about their special habits – whether, for instance, the eight-month-old likes to be picked up and brought downstairs for a cuddle in front of the television when he wakes or whether his mother usually rocks him back to sleep by jiggling the cot. Ask what kind of stories they like read to them, and what games they usually play before being tucked in.

This kind of concern for small children will impress the parents, and they are much more likely to trust you than, say, the don't-care girl next door who plays her favourite records so loudly she wouldn't even hear the baby bawling its head off.

Some parents with small sons, incidentally, welcome a boy sitter, who may often be far more fun with bedtime games. And a three-year-old, some parents notice, can be much more willing to clamber under the blankets if it is an older boy who says it's time to put his head down.

Baby-sitting is an ideal job if you happen to be swotting for exams or have the kind of hobby like sewing, model-making, reading or writing for which your own home is somehow always too noisy and cramped.

But remember also that, humble though it may seem, baby-sitting is one of the most responsible jobs in the world. If you are not used to being with babies or small children, make sure you know the kind of dangers and mischief they can get up to. It may be O K to leave the saucepan handle for your nightly milk drink sticking out from the oven-top at home, but with a three-year-old roaming about it could mean a scalding accident and a trip to hospital. Leaning out of windows, clutching at disinfectant on the kitchen shelf, slamming doors on tiny fingers, lurching about at the top of a flight of stairs – it's all too easy to forget that small children need watching constantly. Even when safely asleep, they should be checked regularly.

Make sure you have the phone number of the place where the parents have gone, or ask them to check back with you during the evening. Know the number of a neighbour or the local doctor in case of any emergency.

A warning: some parents will offer you the freedom of the kitchen and use of anything about the house. Don't abuse their hospitality by emptying the fridge and leaving the washing-up, making costly telephone calls, or scratching their favourite records.

A treasured and trusted baby-sitter will never be short of work. Even if your first employers can only afford to go out once in two months, they will recommend you to all their friends.

B2 BABY-WALKING

One up from pram pushing – and a lot more demanding! In any neighbourhood you are bound to find at least one young mother with a tiny baby, and a son or daughter only a year or so older. She is stuck with feeding schedules and maybe work at home too, just when the eighteen-month-old is at the most adventurous, dangerous, wanting-to-walk stage. Mothers in this situation might be more than grateful for a young neighbour who can guide and guard a toddler with her early stumblings while they concentrate on their other duties. The same applies if they are stuck at home with one child down with chicken-pox or a chill while the other is rarin' to go out to the park. And if you know of small children living near you, who go to the same school or one near by, why not offer to walk them to and from school?

I know one twelve-year-old boy who has baby-walked seven under-threes (one at a time, of course!) for an hour or two at weekends, after school and during holidays and is now so experienced at getting them striding, running, hopping and jumping with barely a bruise that he has a waiting-list! And you should see his racing bike!

When offering yourself for a job like this, you should, naturally, be able to recite the road safety code. And, when you take the little one out, say exactly which park or playground you are going to, and which roads you will be taking.

B3 BEDTIME STORYTELLER

Excellent training if you've ever thought of being an actor or a radio book-reader. This is not such hard work as baby-sitting, and don't expect to be too well paid, but at least it will take only an hour or less out of your evening, and, once your reputation spreads, will steadily add to your savings.

If you like reading out loud, and you get on well with small children, approach any parents you know with under-sevens. A busy mother with a weeks-old baby and two boisterous older children might view you as a visiting angel if you dropped in a few evenings a week for an hour or so when she was grappling with feeding the baby and making the supper, so that you could read the others a few soothing favourite fairy-tales to quieten them down and get them ready for sleep.

If they don't seem to have many books in the house, see if you can rake out some that you enjoyed when you were small, or get them from the library. If this grateful mother starts telling her friends how you've turned her early evenings from bedlam into bliss, you'll be in demand for years ahead! But I would ask for payment by the hour, if I were you. Maybe you will earn a little less if they drop off to sleep quickly, but with the kind of rumbustious family that most needs your talents, the chances are that the half-hour you agreed upon before starting the job could well turn out to be more than double that. There are some who take advantage and ask you to stay on 'just a little bit longer, dear' because, when your thirty minutes are up, the three-year-old is still yelling to know what's going to happen to Paddington Bear in the next chapter and the supper's about to burn. Before you know what's happened, you're being paid half-rate every other evening. So check your watch, and make the point politely – perhaps giving the parent a list of your reading stints at the end of each week.

B4 BIKE REPAIRING

A lot of parents buy their small children bikes and do not teach them how to repair them by themselves. Either they have had no experience of cycling themselves, or they have forgotten whatever they learned, or they are just too busy. And few cycle shops now offer repair services.

If you have a bike of your own, make sure you know how to mend punctures, check brakes, oil sprockets, tighten chains and do all the other cycle-repairing chores. You could build up quite a nice little spare-time business of your own, going round local families mending punctures and doing regular safety checks.

For this job, naturally, you must have a copy of the official cycle safety code and any repair manuals available from local bookshops and cycle shops. Ask your school or club or write to the Royal Society for the Prevention of Accidents. There are also excellent books on bike mending which you could borrow through your local library.

B5 BIKE TRAINING

Know any local tricycling kids rarin' to get going on two wheels, whose parents are too busy to spend afternoons pushing, holding and watching that they don't topple off or go sailing into the main road? Take along your cycle safety code book (which you should be

able to recite by heart) and ask if they would like you to give a hand and teach the children balance and braking and the rules of the road. Check local regulations, but a child's first two-wheeler is usually allowed on park paths – a much easier, safer way to start learning, and not so many grazes when you fall on grass instead of tarmac.

B6 BRANCH-FELLER AND -PRUNER

Well, more a tree-pruner for neighbours, really. If you know any old folk near by with trees that need a bit of lopping and trimming, why not offer your services? You need to have the use of a good sturdy ladder and saw. Your employers may wish to tell you exactly which branches to saw off. If they are unsure, you could ask the advice of your parents if they are knowledgeable gardeners or inquire at your local garden centre. Sometimes the parks superintendent in your area can be very helpful too. Above all, be extremely careful when climbing trees – your employers can't accept liability if you fall and break your leg!

B7 BUTCHER'S HELPER

Fetching and carrying meat from the freezer, laying out and tidying up the meat in a local butcher's shop that is busy on Saturday mornings and a couple of afternoons during the week can be a dependable, well-paid job if you like hard work and don't baulk at the sight of a bit of blood and offal. You will learn how to tidy and rearrange the meat and poultry in the window to make it look more attractive, how to scrub down the chopping-blocks and clean out the display trays, and perhaps how to gut and truss a chicken. And you'll learn, too, how to recognize a piece of well-hung tender meat compared with a hunk of gristle only shortly out of the freezer, which will make you a wise meat shopper for Mum and Dad when they're busy.

C1 CAR CLEANING

Since car-washes have been springing up everywhere, as a young freelance car-washer you have to be especially efficient, or you'll get the door slammed in your face next time you go knocking on doors round the neighbourhood on a Sunday morning. Bring your bucket and washcloths, and charge extra if the owner expects you to provide the detergent and polishes.

Always remember to wash the wheels, too – a hint lots of boys and girls ignore, thinking the owners won't notice. They will! And make sure that there isn't a smear left on the glasswork when you've finished.

C2 CARPET SHAMPOOING

This is the kind of housework ordeal most people loathe – and they are therefore only too happy if you can offer to do it for them. Try it out in your own home first to make sure that you are adept. They may have their own carpet shampooer; otherwise, you could ask your parents if you could borrow theirs, or else it is usually possible to hire one from a nearby hardware shop.

Before starting work, inspect the carpets for stains, and ask what they are. Some don't come out with ordinary shampooing and need a special dry-cleaning lotion you can buy in a tube. You apply this first, allow to dry, then brush out the carpet before starting the cleaning proper. Before stating your charge, it would be wise to check what any local carpet-cleaning firms are demanding.

C3 CAT-CARING

There's quite a lot of cash to be made during the holiday seasons by looking after neighbours' cats when they are away.

Loving owners will be impressed – and probably more generous, too – if you can say that you will pop in twice a day, rather than just once, that you will cook pussy some liver instead of just opening a tin, and that you will give them a nice cuddle and a stroke with their saucer of milk.

C4 CHARRING

An unreasonably maligned job: plenty of well-known actors and actresses have filled in while 'resting' by doing housework. And the old-fashioned full-time trustworthy char is a jewel rarely to be found.

Seek out any working couples in your street block or estate. You can either call and ask if they would like a few hours' cleaning a week, or you can write out (neatly) a few cards detailing your services, and giving your address and phone number. Put one in the local newsagent's window too, perhaps. You can expect to be well paid for work that is thorough and not slapdash. No use just wafting around with the Hoover without moving the chairs, or flicking the duster as if you were waving a flag. And if you show eagerness to do the dirty jobs like cleaning the bathroom and the oven, you should get more generously rewarded. This is the sort of job that comes easier to those dutiful daughters and sons who are used to doing their share of the chores at home.

For this job, especially if you are given a key to go in and clean up while your employers are at work, it goes without saying that you must be scrupulously

honest – also reliable, because there is nothing more irritating for a worn-out working grown-up, expecting sparkling kitchen and pristine bathroom, than to come home instead to a sink full of greasy breakfast dishes and grey-rimmed washbasins.

Many families who can cope with their own indoor cleaning might welcome you for a once-a-year cleaning of all the outdoor paintwork.

C5 CHRISTMAS STOCKING DESIGNING

This is a really profitable at-home job for which you can start taking orders from September onwards. (You could combine this with baby-sitting.)

All families would love to give traditional, decorative stockings laid at the bottom of the bed or beneath the tree on Christmas Eve. Unfortunately, the shops usually offer either cheap, shoddy, sweet-filled socks into which you cannot fit extra presents, or ludicrously expensive affairs.

Yet you don't have to be a nifty stitcher to make really exciting, resplendent Christmas stockings that could earn you a small fortune over the months.

First, invest in materials for two or three prototypes. You'll need some red flare-free nylon net, red felt, red bias binding or tape, orange and white bobbles on a band (used to trim lampshades), some stitch-on sequins and any scraps of wool or ribbon, tinsel or shiny buttons you may have about the house. You can buy all of these from the fabric and haberdashery counters of most large department stores.

To give you an idea for your first effort: double your net and cut out a large stocking shape (larger than you think – imagine the presents having to fit in!). If you draw an oblong fifty centimetres by twenty-five, then chalk or pin the stocking shape inside this area, you will have a reasonable size.

Stitch the double stocking shape together with the red tape. Then cut out a wide strip of red felt to go round the top of the stocking (imagine a wellington boot doubled over). Stitch this. Now comes the fun: decorate the strip of red felt with a line of tinsel tape (or two if you like), plus a line of lampshade bobble tape. Add a sprinkling of sequins.

With a few scraps of red or white wool you could tie two or three bows in the net.

You might, if you are good at embroidery, sew a child's name around the red felt strip or on to a heart, oval or Christmas-tree-shape of felt tacked on to the net fabric.

You may, of course, have lots of better ideas for making a stocking, depending upon the exciting decorative bits and pieces you can find on the haberdashery counter, your local market stall or Mum's ragbag.

Then take your demonstration stocking round to local parents (when the kids are out of sight, of course!) and ask if they would like to commission some. Work out the basic costs of your materials carefully first, check the time it takes you to make the stockings, and allow yourself a modest profit, which should, I'm sure, be considerably less than that offered by the snootier gift shops.

C6 CINEMA USHER

Maybe your local cinema or meeting hall is short-staffed at holiday-times or on busy evenings. Offer your services by writing to, or calling on, the manager.

You will be needed to guide people to their seats – don't flash your torch too far! – and perhaps go round with a tray offering ice-creams and drinks during the interval. Also, report to the manager if there are any trouble-makers in the audience.

If you're a cinema fan and not a fresh-air fiend, this could be just the job for you. A lot of film directors, producers and writers started just this way!

C7 CLIPPING HEDGES

Not everybody has one of those whizzy electric clipping machines. And, especially in the fast-growing spring and summer, gardeners busy warring with weeds and greenfly would more than appreciate an energetic youngster to trim the privet.

Before you start, check that the clippers are sharp. Some thoughtless garden hobbyists are inclined to offer you a rusty relic from the greenhouse, which leaves even the strongest girl or boy a physical wreck before they've got half-way down one side. Offer to take them to be sharpened yourself, for a charge. If you need to borrow Mum or Dad's clippers, expect to be paid more.

C8 COACHING

If you are really good at any academic subject, like maths, English, languages and, most in demand, reading and writing, and possess plenty of patience, there should be quite a few jobs around. Ask any local families if they have a son or daughter who needs a little coaching with schoolwork. Or you could help with piano, violin, flute or guitar practice or ballet lesson rehearsals.

There may be a gap of ten years between coach and pupil, or you could be just one year ahead at school. If you happen to be brilliant on the computer or at the guitar, there's no reason, I suppose, why you shouldn't be paid to coach somebody older than you.

Coaching is much in demand because parents often discover (didn't yours, too, perhaps?) that it's no use Mum or Dad nagging a son or daughter to do swotting or practising. It's a waste of time yelling at kids to go through their French verbs or insisting that they rewrite a scrawled, misspelled English essay if this invariably ends up in abuse and a family row. Also, there are many so-called late developers, who may be bright as buttons, but whose reading and writing is way behind.

This is where somebody else, young, friendly and unemotionally critical but firm, can do wonders. Know what I mean by unemotionally critical? Well, mothers and fathers are all too easily inclined to make an ordinary, lazy mistake into some kind of hereditary disaster and character assassination rolled into one – 'John, only a silly wimp wouldn't be able to answer that question about how a kettle boils dry! You must take after your stupid grandmother . . .!'

You, being a born coach (perhaps talented enough to be a teacher one day?), will simply remark: 'You've seen steam coming out of a kettle hundreds of times, haven't you? This is because water evaporates into the air when it reaches boiling-point, which is 100 degrees Celsius.' No mention of imbecile grannies.

Note the difference in approach? You are telling a small child that he has failed to make one simple observation, forgotten a lesson, maybe because he feels tired or harassed. You are not destroying his self-confidence by accusing him of being a dunce, so he will keep on trying. That's why coaches – even unofficial, junior ones – can sometimes achieve results that amaze their employers. Simple, really. Think about it consciously when you take your first coaching job, because, next to academic know-how, it's the whole secret of success. Plus, needless to say, lots of praise and encouragement for any progress, however slow (Jenny, you've got nine out of ten of those sums right. Very good. Keep on like this and you'll soon be catching up . . .').

It's the same with young ones learning to read and write. Too many parents are taken in by the idea that all intelligent children must be able to read and write before they are five, and so they make learning such a miserable duty that even the brightest refuse to try. Maybe you remember this happening to you, so that you baulked at those boring easy-reader books and read later than your classmates at infant school. If this is the case, so much the better, because you will make a more understanding coach.

By popping in for half an hour or so twice a week or even daily, and guiding your pupils gently, with lots of jokes and no stress, you can help some seemingly backward six- and seven-year-old non-readers and non-writers jump the hurdle within a fortnight. Pupils whose native language is not English – Urdu, Greek or Chinese, for instance – are a bigger challenge, but so should be the reward! Two extra pieces of advice here: if they have been glaring obstinately at boring baby readers, borrow some more sophisticated ones from your local library which they will find more fun.

And stress to parents (show them this book, if you like) that, just because a child has mastered her first sentence, this does not mean she can read or write properly. You will need to continue to help (if less frequently) for a while to establish and broaden her abilities.

Make the point, of course, that you are not a professional tutor, just a young person with whom the child will not feel too frightened or challenged. You would charge more for this than for baby-sitting, naturally, because it can be quite exhausting – noticed how haggard and irritable even the nicest teachers can be at the end of a school day? But, needless to say, you won't charge half as much as a qualified adult.

Sports enthusiasts are also in demand. Plenty of youngsters may welcome some coaching in your specialty, such as tennis, football or swimming (for the latter, of course, you'll need proficiency and life-saving certificates).

C9 COMPETITOR

It's not all Olympic Gold Medals, you know! If you're canny, as they say in Scotland, you can earn quite a few prizes by going in for newspaper and magazine competitions, or those advertised on the labels of groceries from the corner shop or supermarket.

I had a friend who was very hard up, and always got annoyed when he saw on the pack of cheese or biscuits he was unwrapping phrases like 'Your chance to win £500 or a trip to Bermuda . . .'

In fact, it got him so angry that he made a study of media competitions, including television and radio – determined to win. He won enough cash to buy two new tyres for his bike in the first six months, then a holiday for the whole family.

Of course, you need to be quite clever, but don't always go on your teacher's opinion of you. I once interviewed an old lady who was called a dunce when she was at school, who made her living writing letters to newspapers, for which she was paid a pound a time. She was very annoyed with herself if hers was not always top of the page!

The same applies to competitions. Work out the

system, persevere and read the rules. But sort out your own rules, too. However bright you may be, and however neat and inspired your contribution, it's no use if you aren't quick on the uptake. Get the paper first thing in the morning and have your contribution in the afternoon post.

There are some dishonest boys and girls who send in letters with their entries, saying that any winnings will go to help a non-existent crippled brother or granny who hasn't had a holiday for ninety years. I'm afraid the judges are wise to all that!

Often, all that the companies running competitions are doing is getting some bright ideas out of you that they cannot think up themselves. Be cynical. Even if you only get a complimentary prize, follow it up with a plea for a job, if it happens to be an industry that interests you.

It may surprise you that not many fourteen-year-olds, for instance, have the impertinence to write to managing directors telling them that they can suggest slogans for their product and, if they want them, ideas on how to make it more efficient or more marketable. Try this. Keep a copy of your letter and the managing director's reply. If you are still interested in their branch of industry a year later, write again.

You will, I'll bet, enter that office or factory for the first time not with your competition entry or a file of letters, but with that metaphorical silver spoon in your mouth. And well earned, too.

D1 DECORATING

A really tough way of making money. But it's much easier if you come from a home-decorating, do-it-yourself family and therefore know how to wash down and prepare a wall before emulsioning it, how to sand-paper woodwork, prime and undercoat it before

adding the final coat, and how to keep your equipment clean and not leave a mess.

You can earn a lot of money if you build up a reputation for being a good little home decorator. Elderly couples and widowers who are a bit past climbing ladders and rollering ceilings often need just one room done that is not worth the while of a professional decorator.

Can you do wallpapering too? If your parents are papering or you know anybody else who is, go along and watch and learn. It's easy once you know the tricks and if you have patience. But do not offer to do papering until you have tried it yourself at home – maybe your room needs something over all those drawing-pin holes from discarded pin-ups?

Once your decorating offer is accepted, sort out whether your employers are going to supply the materials and equipment. Usually they will. But if a pensioner couple say: 'We'd just like it sort of beige, with a flowery paper over the window wall,' then go round to your local do-it-yourself shop and get colour cards, and ask them to choose exactly which pattern of paper they want. Then, if they want you to buy paint, turpentine, brushes, paper and adhesive, make sure you get receipts for these, so that everything is above-board and honest. Lots of people change their minds about the colour and the paper they've chosen once it's around the room, and this will save them blaming it on you – financially, anyway!

D2 DELIVERING MESSAGES AND SMALL PARCELS

If you have a bike or even a moped (for which you must have a licence), so much the better for this job. A surprising number of small firms need light packages or urgent letters hand-delivered where even express mail would take too long. Either they do not have enough work to employ a full-time delivery man or woman, or else these are on holiday. Maybe, if it is a shop or office on your way home from school, you could arrange to call in daily for any quick journey. Some businesses have special rush weeks – before trade exhibitions or dress shows, or when Christmas deliveries are due to the stores – when you can find yourself with more than enough work.

D3 DELIVERING NEWSPAPERS

Are you an early riser? Got a good alarm clock? Then this is a good steady job spurned by the lazy layabouts who can only bring themselves to crawl out of bed ten minutes before it's time to leave for school.

The earlier you get going on your morning round, the better. There are lots of busy professionals – broadcasters, television directors, researchers and interviewers, journalists and stockbrokers to name but a few – who really need their papers as early as possible. Then you will have time to sit down to a relaxed extra breakfast before setting off for school.

But I would not advise this kind of job for any boy or girl who is working hard for exams. The sheer physical effort can leave you dozy half-way through the morning's lessons and without the energy to complete your homework. Better to offer to do the Sunday-morning stint only, perhaps, or choose another kind of weekend job.

D4 DOG (AND CAT) GROOMING

Luckily, it is usually those bedraggled canines with adorably brown eyes who look as though they've been dragged through a hedge backwards but wouldn't harm a fly who are your happy challenge.

But it is still a good idea to have – or have had – a dog of your own and been friendly with others who need tidying. Some get very tense and snappy, but if you keep calm and gentle they will usually settle down. Some animals like you to get it over with fast, others react better to the slow, soothing approach. And if your expertise with brush and comb is admired on park walks, you soon build up a circle of customers. Knowing about de-fleaing, worming and shampooing helps, and for these extra duties you would get more pay.

Cats are more temperamental and a pair of tough claw-proof gardening gloves comes in useful. But if you love felines (they can tell at a glance!), keep a cat-mint ball and some tasty packets of morsels handy. Transforming an old hearthrug into a catfood ad can be more pleasure than work.

D5 DOG-WALKING

Some dog-lovers are too old and others work all day and are too tired at night to give their pet an evening stroll.

A young person who can offer to take a beloved animal out for a half an hour's exercise around the park or over the common every day after school may expect only a modest wage. But it's a dependable one, and the work's not too arduous either. You can be taking some fresh air, too, and even if you aren't working out your English essay in your mind, you could be looking forward to ways of spending your earnings. This can be a more than pleasant job if you cannot have a dog of your own and happen to be very fond of them.

Make sure you know the dog's personality before you take it out. Should it always be on the leash? If not, when and where will the owners allow you to let it run free? It probably won't ever happen, but ask them to tell you what to do if the dog disappears and won't return to your constant calling or whistling. It's always best to get emergency situations sorted out first, and then you won't have recriminations if accidents or incidents do happen.

As with children, call first and spend a little time playing with the dog so that it knows you.

D6 DOLL-MAKING

If you are nifty with a needle, this is a great money-maker for birthday and Christmas presents for under-fours.

You have to buy your own fabric and decorative accessories, of course, but this can become a very profitable at-home occupation, like Christmas stockings.

First, get out any books on stuffed toys and dolls you can find in your local library and study them. Also, have a look in local bookshops – they may have some that, if you cannot afford to buy, you could order from your library. Ask the chief librarian – he or she will usually be very helpful. Go through your Mum's magazines and sewing books and you might find several how-to-make instructions for dolls and toys without having to go to any further bother.

Then, having decided which basic doll you want to make (you can always change the faces and clothes),

collect your equipment. First, the stuffing (got any old cushions filled with plastic foam scraps nobody wants any more?) and the strong cotton body material. Then, three-ply wool for the hair (know any knitters with left-overs?), embroidery thread for eyes, nose, mouth, eyebrows. Felt, perhaps, for the shoes. Lots of fabric off-cuts and discarded old clothes to make tiny doll gear. Orange hair, gingham shirt and jeans cut from your brother's throwaways for a boy doll, perhaps. Black plaits, red pinafore dress and white blouse for a girl, maybe. It can be really exciting giving personality to your dolls and making them different. If they're sewn really carefully, you'll have no end of customers.

As with making Christmas stockings, when buying materials seek out shops which sell off-cuts cheaply. You might find it worth while, if you get lots of orders, to buy up several yards of heavy white cotton, then dye it pink and/or brown, or one big bag of plastic foam pieces for stuffing. Take your time working out the cost of making your dolls, so that both sides are happy when you charge. Check the prices of the plastic dolls in the local shops, and then you can tell your would-be customers that you can make them a doll that is unique.

If you are skilled, you can try to make the dolls' features, as well as their clothes, to specifications to suit your customers. Maybe a boy doll for the birthday of a two-year-old daughter who is jealous of her new-born brother, so she can bash that instead of him!

And not just dolls, of course. You can make teddy bears, elephants, hedgehogs, owls – the whole animal kingdom. Or how about puppets?

And when you are asking around, remember that there are plenty of aunties and grans, not to say uncles, who would probably order one or two from you.

D7 DOLL'S HOUSE BUILDING AND FURNISHING

Any good at carpentry? Have you still got an adored doll's house of your own?

This is an area where, perhaps, two boys and/or girls might get together. One builds the doll's house and the other paints and furnishes it.

Start, as with other spare-time enterprises like this, with your prototype. With any luck you may find some blockboard in the toolshed, some leftovers in the paint pots from last year's decorating and some odd bits of carpeting. Use your imagination to make and paint tiles for the roof, use thick plastic for the windows and tiny bits of cotton or nylon lace for curtains. Matchboxes on matchsticks might make a table. Could you convert another matchbox into a miniature TV set? There's nothing wrong with doing a bit of cheating with your home-made effort, however, and searching the best local toyshop for doll's furniture and those little toy plates of food. Though, if you are good at modelling, you could try making them yourself.

This is the kind of spare-time job that will probably turn out to be a lifetime's hobby. The sort of job that requires creativity as well as practical common sense.

First, having decided this is the kind of spare-time earning you would like to embark upon, go round as many toy museums and posh toyshops as you can, making notes and drawings of the doll's houses you see. Maybe you know some friends with doll's houses you've admired. Ask if you can make plans of them, copy the furnishings and architecture. You will find that the most popular design is a two-storey, four-roomed house with the whole of the frontage attached by hinges, so that it swings open to show the inside.

Although you may be able to make use of lots of free fabric, wallpaper and carpet scraps, you will probably spend quite a lot on glue and paint, not to say endless time on the actual work. But building doll's houses will give enormous pleasure to the sort of meticulous young person who likes making miniature things, and you should make quite a considerable profit from your careful glueing and painting too.

It wouldn't be a bad idea to make up two or three doll's houses: for instance, a one-storey, two-roomed thatched cottage, with real straw roof, and furniture made of twigs and sawn-off bits of a sapling trunk; a two-storey conventional home, with two bedrooms, sitting-room and bathroom; why not a tiny holiday villa in its surroundings, all on a cheap tin tray bought in your local discount shop? You could make a red-tiled roof from painted bits of egg boxes, get some sand from the pet shop or a nearby builder's pile, and use a carton painted with blue oil-paint and filled with water for the swimming-pool. Add your own tiny palm trees and tropical flowers. Maybe your builders' merchants have got a few leftovers of those tiny mosaic wall tiles, which would make good paving-stones for a patio.

You can probably think up many more ideas yourself – even, perhaps, copying a customer's own house!

Make your house as sturdy as you can – remember that it will be played with. And there is nothing more disappointing for small children than to find their present collapsing when they are moving round the furniture.

D8 DRESSMAKING

If you enjoy making your own clothes, this could grow into an all-the-year-round spare-time occupation.

Lots of women have a favourite dress, top or pair of trousers which is fast wearing out, and which they cannot find stocked anywhere in the shops. Maybe it's the colour, the cut or the design that specially appeals to them and flatters their looks and shape.

If they happen to be hopeless at sewing, while you are adept at your family machine, why not suggest that you become one of those old-fashioned round-the-corner home dressmakers who, forty years ago, were much respected and greatly in demand. Wealthy women who discovered a dressmaker who was clever at fitting and darting and offered wise inspiration on the choice of colours and styles kept her a closely guarded secret from all but the very best friends!

You can dressmake in two ways: either straight from a pattern or by unpicking the favourite dress and making a paper pattern from it, so that it can be made again.

If you're using a pattern, get your customer to choose it, together with the fabric and trimmings. You might offer advice here on the choice of thread; for instance, a man-made stretch fabric will need a polyester thread, otherwise, however well sewn by you, the seams will be continually coming apart. Take a look at the pattern and instructions together first and check your customer's measurements. It is better to have rather too much fabric than too little – skimping can turn out a tragedy when you end up with only one sleeve. Although you can agree to buy the accessories (not forgetting to keep the receipts), insist that your customer choose the material herself, even if you go along with her to advise. It is useless, you may know, to buy a stretch fabric for a pattern that calls for non-stretch material, but she may not realize this unless you tactfully see that she re-reads the instructions.

However professional-looking your own wardrobe may be, filled with dresses and suits made with quite complicated button-holing, gathered sleeves and pockets, be sure that your first efforts for others are ultra-simple.

You may have a lot of trouble making your own pattern from an existing dress (unpicking, then pressing out the pieces and laying them on newspaper or brown paper to make your pattern), but at least you should have less trouble with the darting and fitting, since you know it fits already. But be *extra careful* that you check you are laying the different bits of the patterns at the correct angle on the material. This may mean that you will need more fabric than at first seems apparent. In a dress factory, they will probably use one roll of material to cut out all the sleeves for a dozen dresses, another roll for the bodices and a third for the skirts, thus saving several yards. You won't be able to do this, and if you slot in a sleeve diagonally when it should be straight to the fold or selvedge, your attempt could be a disaster and you will find yourself not only out of a job, but probably owing some money too.

But having issued these warnings, I can tell you a story of a fifteen-year-old friend who was given a smashing pair of trousers by her aunt, who had put on too much weight to squeeze into them any more. They were very expensive and flattering, comfortable to wear because of an elasticized waistline and – to her pleasure and astonishment – turned out to have only two seams. When hers began to get shiny at the knees and frayed along the bottoms, she unpicked them, made her own pattern and found that from cutting out to adding the last finishing-off stitches took her less than three hours. Within a fortnight she had made three more in different colours for her holiday. An admiring neighbour, just a couple of inches taller and wider round the hips, asked if she could run a couple up for her too, because she wasn't the build for jeans. Within weeks she was inundated with orders, including several for a simple cotton smock that she also copied. She has kept in business by refusing to make identical tops, trousers or evening gowns for her clients. With a simple pattern but different kinds of fabric, different prints and different trimmings, you would never know they had the same beginnings.

If you are not all that confident of your sewing expertise, why not start by making children's clothes? Little girls' dresses are very easy, but you will find there is quite a lot of competition from factory-made tots' clothes in the shops. Go through the pattern books and try and find some really original designs. Search the fabric counters for cheap, unusual materials that you haven't seen in the dress shop windows. Another idea is children's sunhats or painting smocks.

You might try hostess aprons for anybody you know who is giving a special dinner party. Make them longish, of a luxury material to match the evening dress your customer will be wearing. Many women have a basic long black gown or trouser suit, and a hostess apron, though easy to make, could spice it up a bit. Make suggestions – like white spotted voile, for instance, some exotic sari silk, or even gingham. A rather hard-up but enterprising Scots girl I know has had the same black dress for the past five years, with which she wears a succession of tartan aprons or sleeveless over-smocks.

The best way to advertise is to go round and ask relatives, friends or neighbours if they would like anything made, wearing the outfit of which you are most proud, so that they can see what kind of standards to expect of you. Then offer to revisit for a longer chat, taking with you any magazine cut-outs or patterns you can collect to help them to make up their minds. But don't be too ambitious. Don't risk anything like draping, for example, or tricky pleating.

You may think you know the necessary ABCs of sewing, or can lean on your Mum for advice. But it is still a good idea to invest in one of the several excellent simple how-to-do-it sewing books available in any good bookseller's or through a women's magazine.

As to what to charge, your clothes should be quite a bit cheaper than if bought from a shop. But if a customer doesn't seem too hard up, and is really desperate to have a frock copied, and you can make yours look quite as good as the original, then you can fairly charge the price originally paid.

F1 FARM WORK

This could be anything from pea-picking to potato-lifting, harvesting, sheep-dipping, driving a tractor or helping with the milk.

You need to be in good physical condition, boy or girl. If you're city-bred, don't forget that the bane of farm life for you may be not so much the back-breaking work as the flies and midges. Take plenty of insect repellent with you, plus disinfectant and calamine lotion in your first-aid box if you are going to stay on a farm for a few days or weeks. And comfortable shoes – better three old pairs of plimsolls that

you are used to and can throw away when you go home than some brand new footwear that turns out to pinch and blister when you have to do a lot of walking in the heat.

If you don't know of a farm, ask around – your teachers or local youth club might be able to help – and buy any farming papers, which often carry ads for holiday help wanted. It's a much healthier and more socially useful way of developing muscles and a good physique than any judo course.

If you have not had a tetanus injection recently, check with your doctor. He or she may advise one as a precautionary measure in case you get a cut or put a fork prong through your foot (heaven forbid!).

F2 FETCHING AND CARRYING SHOPPING

Plenty of well-off pensioners and working people will be happy to give you a nice tip for taking their list along to the local shops and buying their groceries for them.

For this you need to be scrupulously honest and recommended by your parents. Always check the shopping list and choice of shops with your employer first. If you happen to know that Store A is selling frozen peas cheaper than Store B, and tell her so, she will be more than pleased to ask for your assistance again. If you can say that you always check vegetables for freshness and look at the date stampings on perishable plastic-packed foods like sausages or cream, she will be impressed, but make sure you do it!

Always get a receipt for everything. You cannot guarantee that the onion in the middle of the pack is not mildewy at the core, but you can prove that you are totally honest. Here, as always, this is the most reliable way of earning money and friends.

If you are shopping for an old person who you know is short of money, be generous and do the job for a pittance. But make sure you are not being taken in by a miser. Chatting up the neighbours ('I'm just going to get the shopping for Mr Robertson. Does he usually have such a heavy load of shopping?') can give you a clue. If he has all the luxuries, then he can pay you just over the going wage, can't he?

F3 FISH-FEEDING

Like other pets, people get devoted to their fish, and need someone to look after them when they go on holiday. You can either take the fish into your own home, or go in to see to them daily.

The most important rule to follow is: too little fish-food rather than too much. And, without being morbid, if one of the darling goldfish belonging to a dear old lady floats to the top while she's off on her annual fortnight to her sister, I would advise the kindly solution of buying her another, looking as much the same as possible, and welcome her without so much as a mention of the sad death. It may take half your earnings, but you'll feel the reward in other ways, won't you?

F4 FISHING FLIES

Fishing is one of the most popular sports in the world, and fly fishing is considered the most aristocratic. Fishermen will spend as much in a week as you'd splurge on clothes or your bike for those funny little tied up bits of feather, hair, thread and hook. If you decide to make fishing flies you will have to invest

some savings on a vice and materials, but once you get the knack it's easy, and you will soon have paid for your outlay a dozen times over.

For those who enjoy fishing, this is a meticulous occupation for the time of year when it's out of season. But if you want to, you can be making flies at home in your own time all year round!

First, collect all the fishing books you can from your library and ask your local fishing shop for advice. If you're a fishing enthusiast yourself, you're on your way.

Find out from your local fishing shop or any fishing friends and neighbours which are the most popular flies on the nearby or most popular rivers and reservoirs, lakes or lochs. Then look up the name and address of your local fishing club, and ask if you can put up a notice on their board offering to sell home-made flies.

Once you've swotted up enough information, you might even add a little leaflet to go with a collection of six flies, explaining, for instance, how your Black Witch is best at sundown on the north side of a popular fishing river not many miles away. Mind you, it also helps if you can boast a snapshot of yourself holding up a magnificent trout caught with one of your own flies!

As for what to charge for your flies, this will be crafty guesswork, as there's a lot of magic and superstition in fishing. If your first sales do well, you're on to a winner!

F5 FIXING THINGS

Sounds vague, but if you are handy with a screwdriver, gimlet, spanner and power-drill, jobs that may seem impossible to people who are not do-it-yourself-inclined can be easy, well paid and much appreciated. Jobs like fixing shelves and wall fittings of every kind, and refitting all those wall fittings they've put in shoddily which have fallen out. You may need to do some making good first, and there are a number of new products on the market now to ensure that picture-hangers, wall lights, tin-openers and all the other paraphernalia people like to stick around their rooms will not topple out.

Here again, it is best if you have a parent, neighbour or relative who is a professional (far too busy for small jobs), and who could guide you if you ask nicely and give some help in return.

You cannot charge anything like the professional rates for the job, however well you may do it. State straight away what knowledge and experience you have – 'I've helped my uncle, who is a builder, for the past two summer holidays' would be a very good reference, for example.

Be very careful about measuring up and assessing how much work will be involved before you come to any agreement. This is why professional handymen always submit what they call estimates, because a job can be far more complicated and take up more time than appears at first glance. There are some mean-minded adults who will assure you how easy it is to bracket a heavy mahogany shelf on to their frail plasterboard wall, and then go round and complain to your parents about your delinquency when it inevitably collapses.

However eager you may be to get the job, state any doubts you have. And if you think it's too difficult for you or just plain impossible for anybody, for that matter, much better to say so and call it a day.

Also, if your customers want you to buy the materials, get them to agree first which wood, screws, varnish, adhesive, etc. they want. And make sure that you get a receipt for them.

Fixing things sounds easy, but it is one of the more difficult spare-time tasks. You need a lot of persistence as well as practical knowledge. But if you can manage it, you will be one of the most sought-after young persons in your street.

F6 FRUIT PICKING AND BASKETING

This, of course, is seasonal, but usually quite remunerative, since orchard farmers are often desperate to get fruit picked before it becomes over-ripe. Cherries, plums, apples, pears and grapes all need picking, and so do strawberries and tomatoes.

As with general farmwork, ask around and quiz teachers and club leaders. If you live in a city or town, whenever you go for a drive in the country, note down the names of orchards which look as though they could do with pickers when the fruit is ready, and write them a note offering your services. Perhaps they could give you accommodation with a couple of friends, or you could camp near the farmhouse. Especially in August and September, wasps are on every tree, so buy one of the excellent anti-histamine spray-ons from any chemist because you'll be lucky to escape a sting.

G1 GARAGE HELPER

If you like fiddling about with engines, you should have no bother finding a job helping out in a local garage for a few hours a week. It's dirty work and cold in the winter, and your parents will probably spend a bomb on soap and washing-powder, but it will stand you in good stead if you have aspirations about training to be an engineer. And even if you haven't, won't it be satisfying, when you have a car of your own, to know what to do when things go wrong under the bonnet, rather than be charged heavens knows how much for goodness knows what when it chokes to a stop on the motorway!

G2 GARDENING

This includes general jobs, rather than specific ones listed separately in this chapter, for example dead-heading roses, weeding, pruning; clipping overgrown shrubs, clematis or honeysuckle, digging, hoeing and watering – in other words, generally tidying up. The autumn is usually a popular time for selling your energies.

It helps if one of your parents – or at least some adult you know quite well – is a gardener, and can give you a few hints. Employers would not be pleased if you enthusiastically weeded out their carefully nurtured zinnia seedlings! And just to make sure that you will not ravage the wisteria in mistake for the privet they want dug out, collect any free gardening catalogues on offer at your local gardening centre. A couple of evenings leafing through them, and you will soon be able to identify the different plants, and even offer advice on their care.

G3 GOLFING CADDY (AND BALL-FINDER)

This is slave labour – running around picking up little white balls and wheeling along hefty bagfuls of equipment, usually for over-corpulent gentlemen! But, though becoming more and more popular, it is still a game that attracts the well-off, so if you have a snooty golf club near you, try for a job there and you might find yourself handsomely tipped at the end of a morning, and perhaps meet a famous personality or millionaire into the bargain!

If you can't be a caddy, offer to retrieve the balls. The clubhouse will tell you the going price for those returned, and if it's learners' day on the tees, you'll be surprised how much you can pocket.

G4 GUITAR TUITION

Would-be players with serious musical ambitions prefer to go to a professional tutor.

But there are plenty of boys and girls who simply want to be minstrel strummers, the song and dance of the party or camp fire. You will have had some lessons yourself – or happen to be the star of your school concerts. Some pop stars can't read music, but that is their loss. Invest in some song sheets or books. Do parents and neighbours a favour and include a few tunes that are not too cacophonous at practice time. You might suggest a pre-party repertoire to keep the old folk in a benevolent mood.

H1 HARVESTER

Another specialized farming job, which you can often land with a day's notice, depending upon the weather. Maybe there are some fields just a mile or so away from your holiday cottage or caravan, and you're getting a bit bored? Again, take precautions against harvest bugs: they're the nastiest biters of all.

H2 HERB GROWER

Have you got green fingers? Do plants flourish on your windowsill or in your patch of the back garden where those of others wilt and die?

You could make a surprisingly good income during the spring and summer by growing herbs and selling them, especially if your Mum and Dad have a greenhouse and would let you make use of a corner. Otherwise you can still get your seeds growing on your windowsill, especially with the aid of one of those plastic seed-propagating boxes.

Herbs sold in plant shops in the high season cost a bomb, and in many neighbourhoods they are impossible to buy. Yet more and more families are trying out the old-fashioned and unusual herbs as well as the more common ones in their cooking. Here are a few for you to start growing: mint, chives, parsley, marjoram, thyme, rosemary, dill, fennel, basil, chervil, borage, sage and lemon balm.

Start by reading up any books you can find on growing herbs – free from a gardening centre or from your library. Then, before Christmas, send for the seeds you have chosen to grow. Invest in some seeding and potting compost and plenty of little herb pots from your savings or Christmas cash. Follow the instructions on the seed packets.

It's fashionable to say that if you speak kindly to your seeds they will grow all the better. Actually, it just means that if you say so much as a 'Good Morning' to them every day, you will not forget the watering or thinning out!

You can grow some herbs by taking a root or cutting. If you've got a nice bed of mint in your garden, ask if you can pull up a few trailing strands and root them in your pots. Try taking cuttings of rosemary, sage, marjoram and thyme, and put six of each dipped in rooting powder into compost-filled pots. Don't despair if they don't take – try again.

Another very popular culinary flavouring – though not strictly a herb – is bay. Have you got a bay tree in your garden? If so, try a few cuttings from this, too. Or you might even invest in a bay bush, plant it, and then sell off the leaves during the summer.

When your seedlings have sprouted and you are potting them out, the salesmanship begins. Your parsley and basil, both difficult to grow, may not have thrived, but never mind. Sort out whatever healthy plants you have, then look up everything interesting you can about them – some books say borage is supposed to cure everything from a headache to the gout! Anyway, copy down all the information about each herb that you will have for sale. Then write it out neatly on several cards – decorated, perhaps, with a drawing of the herb. At the bottom of your list, give your name, address and the prices per pot of each. (Check the prices at the local gardening shops – or ask how much herbs will be when they come in – then make yours just a bit cheaper). Go round asking for orders, showing your cards.

When the herbs are really flourishing and ready for delivery, buy a pack of cocktail sticks, cut some plain card into oblongs and label them neatly, and impale them on the sticks, putting one into each pot. If you have your own bay tree, offer packets of, say, ten leaves.

You never know – in a couple of seasons, you may be able to afford your own greenhouse!

H3 HOLIDAY CAMP HELPER

This includes two different kinds of job, really. You could be a helper in a family holiday camp – a collection of chalets and caravans – tidying litter, cleaning the washing facilities, helping in the camp shop, getting chalets ready for the next occupants, or even perhaps acting as guard at the swimming pool if they have one (and if you have your life-saving certificate).

Or you could be a leader in a children's holiday camp. This would be far less well paid – in fact, you might only get your board and food – but, for someone who likes being with young ones, much more fun. Here you would have a lot more responsibility: seeing the kids don't get involved in any accidents; that there's no bullying; and that those suffering from homesickness get the comfort they need.

For this, you would need experience of camping yourself, of course – all the know-how from how to make a campfire (and, just as important, how to stop a campfire from spreading!) to how to keep everybody happy inside a tent when it's near freezing and pelting with rain outside. Either write to the camps you have attended or ask at your school or library for a list of camping organizations. But make your application as early as possible. November isn't too soon to approach, say, a boating and canoeing camp (because this happens to be your favourite hobby) to inquire if they would like a helper for a few weeks during the summer holidays.

If you are a naturalist, an ecological enthusiast or a fossil collector, there are several children's organizations which have weekend or even one-day outings throughout the year. They would be more than happy to have a responsible young enthusiast around to encourage the kids and see they don't get into trouble.

H4 HOME HAIRDRESSER (*see also* SHAMPOOER)

This is a quite different way of earning money from helping out at the local hairdressing salon, which is how so many girls earn their first pin money. You do the shampooing, cutting, tinting, perming and blow-drying for relatives, friends and neighbours in their own homes.

You will have no difficulty finding young mums or old ladies who have neither the time nor the money to sit for hours in a salon. Maybe they've got a baby round the place. Maybe they are too frail to get out a lot. Offer a reasonable charge, and they will look upon you as a ministering angel!

But you *must* swot up on the job. If Mrs Brown's copper blonde turns into lawn green after your first visit, every possible client around will don a headscarf at the very sight of you! Write to all the well-known hair preparation firms you can think of – you can list the names and addresses from the packets on the chemist's shelf – and ask for any hair care advice leaflets they have.

These offer lots of very useful advice, and stress the importance of following the instructions of the different brands of tints and perms *exactly*. With some, it doesn't matter if you leave a solution on the hair another couple of minutes while you are chatting, but with others it can be a disaster if you don't check the second hand on your watch.

Unless you know how to cut hair reasonably well (perhaps you have a friend or relative who is a trained hairdresser and has passed on some of the tricks and talents of the trade), don't even offer to try.

Be absolutely open about what you do know and don't know about hairdressing, and make sure that, if your customers want a trim, they realize that you are not in any way qualified. To pretend to be so would be dishonest and, if that poodle-cut a girl pleaded for turned out more like a sheepdog pulled through a hedge backwards, would land you in lots of hot unsoapy water!

Always sterilize any brushes, combs or scissors you use between customers. Simply leave them for a few minutes in a strong solution of disinfectant. If you notice that one of your customers has dandruff, tell her, and suggest a special shampoo for the next session.

If you get pleasure out of doing other people's hair –

you like rearranging and setting not just your own, but your sister's and your Mum's, perhaps – this is a really enjoyable way of paying for some new clothes in your wardrobe.

And if you have a special flair for styling, even better. You've probably got lots of ideas of your own, but why not cut out any appealing newspaper or magazine hairstyles and glue them on to a large sheet of cardboard to help clients decide upon the style they would like?

A conscientious home hairdresser will also want her efforts to enhance the customer's attractions. But a lot of women who would like you to do their hair at home are probably a bit uncertain about how they want it styled. And this is where you could really use your talents and make them grateful to you for a lifetime.

A young woman with three small children, perhaps, and a husband on the dole who has at long last landed himself a nice job. Since the first was born, she's washed her hair in the cheapest, harshest shampoo and hunked at it occasionally with the nail scissors. It is fine and fair and always falls out of sets within hours, and she has a rather square-shaped face. What would you suggest to her? To eat well, use a gentler shampoo plus a conditioner, and to let it grow for a few months until you can give her a pudding-basin cut that you blow-dry with a brush so that it curves around her cheeks and hides her wide jawline.

What would you suggest to a small-headed, short and plump middle-aged neighbour? Now her combed-down hair-do makes her face look like the top end of a pear – you need to bring her hair up and out to make her head look larger, which will distract attention from her waistline. This is where you need to set a shortish style with big curls on the top and sides.

Then what about the depressed ex-teacher in her seventies, with steel-grey hair scraped into a miserable bun? A nice lady, who needs cheering up and getting out of herself a bit? Why not a straight front parting, a fringe and the rest cut just below the ears? It might startle the locals into realizing that she is no pensioner relic and give her a new lease of life. Not to say more work for you, too!

If you are starting from scratch, it might be a good idea to write out a few notices on blank postcards and drop them through the letterboxes of those who look in need of a convenient at-home hair-do. State your experience and abilities, available hours, name, address and telephone number, plus your average charges (or write 'fees to be arranged' if you want to make it cheaper for the pensioner and double for the better-off young wives). Decorate with coloured felt-pen borders and maybe several hairstyled heads. If you aren't good at drawing, perhaps a friend would help.

If there is no nearby salon, or the local one is invariably packed and charges outrageous prices, you could be on to a good thing here. You might even consider going into partnership with a friend.

And don't discard the fact that there are a lot of young men around with flowing locks who would pay for a shampoo and set too. If you haven't got a partner with her blue belt in judo, you'd better get your parents' permission for them to come round to your place for the treatment!

H5 HOTEL (OR BOARDING HOUSE) CHAMBERMAID OR 'BOOTBOY'

This job involves a certain amount of dull, back-aching drudgery – just the same old daily routine of making

beds, changing linen, cleaning baths and basins, hoovering carpets and dusting dressing-tables. But it can be lots of fun – making new friends, going to new places, learning a new language, maybe, or improving your classroom accent. Getting the chance, perhaps, to take morning tea or coffee to some famous faces.

Lots of enterprising young city people get working holiday jobs in beauty-spot hotels during the high season. Though you cannot expect to be paid much, you'll have the advantage of quite a bit of free time, as well as your food and board. And, much as you may love your parents and your home, it's good to get away occasionally, isn't it?

Two girls I know get a four- to six-week summer job on the Continent every year. The first, last year, was in the lovely seaside resort of Positano, in Southern Italy, helping a family who rented out self-catering apartments as well as running their own *pensione*. They were not nervous, because they were travelling and working together. It would have been, they say, a bit frightening for a girl on her own, even meeting their employers beforehand.

Although they worked hard from 7 a.m. to 1 p.m. and then from 6 p.m. for another two hours, the rest of their time was free and they came home with some fabulous straw hats and sun-tans to match. Next summer they plan to go to Spain or France, and they are currently thinking up ways and means of getting to know a hotelier in St Tropez, Majorca or Corfu.

There is really no such job as bootboy any more – he was the lackey who polished the shoes that hotel guests left outside their bedroom doors until he could see his face in them. You won't be needed to do that, but there are hotels that need a youngster ready to do the heavier, menial tasks – carrying luggage, doing the rougher cleaning and gardening, and working the hotel petrol pump. You might get the chance to help with the boats if the hotel is in a fishing or sailing centre, act as a lifeguard if it has a swimming pool, or help with the horses, if it offers riding.

I1 ICE-CREAM VAN HELPER

If you have one or two ice-cream vans circulating in your vicinity, why not ask if they would like a bit of help during the high-demand hot weather? This could be during the summer holidays or after school and at weekends during any heatwave. Give your name, address and phone number. Assure them that you are not only diligent, but also hygiene-conscious (perhaps you have already taken a special course at school, for which you have been awarded high marks).

You may be needed to hurry out of school to meet the van, getting straight to work (after thoroughly scrubbing your hands, of course) to catch those dawdling home with money to spend.

At holiday-times you'll probably be busy touring streets and estates with that familiar ting-a-ling that may sound welcome to those desperate for a cornet but might give you a headache after four solid ear-shattering hours!

12 INVENTING

This is not actually an earning job that offers immediate rewards, if any. But, if there's no quick money around, and you've got an active brain, you could do worse than sit down or go for a walk and think up something useful. Nobody had thought of folding sitting furniture until a ship's carpenter invented the deckchair in 1864. He became a millionaire, renting them out in parks. And what about Percy Shaw, who died in 1976? He was driving home one night and, feeling annoyed because the old-fashioned tramlines which reflected his car's headlights had been removed, took just two minutes to think of the cat's-eye – a system of reflecting glass embedded in the centre of the road to help night motorists. He lived on that spur-of-the-moment inspiration for the rest of his life. Lots of the best inventions have come from young people.

Rules for the would-be inventors:

1. Make a list of what people want, but can't get. Well, can you think of a way of never having to clean windows? A device that, unlike ear-plugs,

keeps out traffic noise but would alert your mum if Gran had a relapse?

2. Once you think you've got an original, a winner, ask the advice of somebody you trust absolutely. They may well tell you P. Smith thought of that in 1892 and it got nowhere. So you'll just have to think again!
3. Get any likely-sounding idea patented *immediately*. Great brains often think alike! Send a dated, addressed letter describing your invention in detail to the Patents Office in London, which will register your claim. Then, if anybody else comes along with the same idea, you can legally state that you thought it up first.

13 IRONING

Have you ever heard the old song: 'Dashing away with the smoothing iron . . .'? It was an old-fashioned joke, because this must be the most loathed household chore of them all. And now that laundries are few and far between and raising their prices almost weekly, lots of busy working families find it a more burdensome pile every week.

If you are a painstaking person and are content to get on with a chore like this while thinking your own thoughts, you may be able to earn a sizeable addition to your savings over the weeks, especially if you make a weekly arrangement with one, two or even three households. Offer to iron the weekly wash for any busy working wives or bachelors you know. Show them a shirt you have ironed as an example of your care and capability.

But, before you set to upon their crumpled pile, make sure that you are familiar with their kind of iron, and check that the thermostat works. What to charge?

Ask your mum what she would be willing to pay if she earned what you guess they are making, but don't over-charge yourself out of a good pocket-money living.

Incidentally, if asked by a bachelor or man on his own to do his shirts in his house or flat, and you're in any way doubtful about the situation, insist that you do them in your own home. Charge more, of course, part of which will go to your parents for the electricity bill and use of the iron.

J1 JACK- OR JILL-OF-ALL-TRADES

Maybe you don't think you have a flair for anything in particular, but if you've always been helpful around the house, you could be a godsend to elderly or overworked neighbours.

Simply make a list of the chores you can tackle reasonably efficiently – from cleaning windows to scrubbing floors and from scouring ovens to cleaning gutters and leaf-blocked drains. Some of the jobs are mentioned separately in this chapter, but your list could be endless. Just ask your parents how many different domestic duties they tackle during one week.

Then prepare a dozen advertisements, neatly penned on plain postcards. You could start them off something like this:

NEED A PAIR OF WILLING HANDS
OCCASIONALLY?
Boy/girl aged —, used to doing all the
jobs below, would like to earn pin-money.

Then add your name, address and phone number.

As people who need this kind of help are often a bit harassed and disorganized, it's a good idea to push your card through their letterbox, then call the next day or weekend, at what you consider to be the most convenient time for them (*not* when they're putting the baby to bed or taking their afternoon snooze), when they have been able to consider your offer.

If you are not sure how much to charge, ask them what they are prepared to pay, and then say that you had better check with your parents whether this would be reasonable. For odd jobs, it seems wise to go on payment by the hour.

K1 KNITTER

Some like it, some loathe it. But girls, or boys, who have advanced beyond the plain-and-purl stage and can click away at cable-stitch while watching television or listening to records could put their flair to good use.

Know of any babies on the way? Then you've got prospective customers in the offing – mother-to-be will probably struggle along with her own grubby, holey effort, but there should be some grandmothers, aunties, work friends and neighbours who would be relieved to pay you to knit a pair of little bootees, vest or jacket. And if it's an autumn- or winter-born baby, point out that woolly bonnets are often forgotten among the baby gifts in our more centrally heated times, yet are just as important as ever.

You may have noticed that the old-fashioned shawl has made a big comeback, not just for old ladies, but for stylish young women too. And it can be made in all sorts of exciting wools and colours, from lacy, near-diaphanous white wrap-arounds, to grace a summer's night out, to heavyweight, brightly coloured plaids that could keep you snug in a howling gale. Knitted hats and caps, too, are always appearing on the fashion pages. You just have to keep up with the style.

And, of course, you could knit bedspreads. The most popular are the traditional ones made of small squares knitted separately and then sewn together, which is an easier task for you if you have only, say, half an hour or so to spare each evening. But there are lots of other designs, too – like a knitted circle, oval or star-shape stitched on to a bedspread-sized piece of material.

If you are creative, you might think up a few ideas, sketch them as best you can, and show them to any prospective buyers. If you are a knitting family, you probably have lots of bits of wool in different colours to give them something to choose from. Otherwise, see if you can get hold of some swatch cards. Ask at your local shop, and write to all of the leading knitting firms. They are usually most helpful, sending leaflets containing ideas plus brochures of their colour ranges and kinds of wool. Libraries, bookshops and newsagents will have books and magazines that may be worth borrowing or buying if you spot some patterns you'd like to try and you think would appeal.

L1 LAUNDERETTE SERVICER (*see also* WASHPERSON)

Another time-consuming job that those without washing-machines find an awful drag.

Old people who can manage a few paces on their own two feet love to take their washing to the launderette because it's a great gossiping place, so it's little use approaching them for work. But working mothers, or those with small children, often with one sick in bed, would gladly tip you generously to haul their load along, dump it in, see it through, and return it.

O K, so it's boring. Well, take a good book, your knitting or your sketching-block. But check the washing rules carefully before you start. You may just have toted along with a grown-up before, and not really noticed when to put in the soap, what change you need for the dryer, and so on. Nor that some clothes can only take a warm wash or medium dry. Sort this out with your employer first.

And *never* pop out of the launderette while the stuff is washing, spinning or drying. There are some launderette thieves who sit quietly in corners looking out for people who nip out for a paper or a bag of sugar between soapings, and snatch a couple of costly anoraks within seconds before anybody has noticed. I know one unfortunate thirteen-year-old who had his pocket money stopped for six weeks when this happened while he shot round the corner for a comic.

L2 LAWN MOWER, TRIMMER, LAYER AND PATCHER

This is a seasonal earner, for late spring and early summer when the grass needs cutting once every three days if it is to look good.

The time to offer your services is when you notice the grass is first beginning to spring up after the cold months. Try to arrange a contract whereby you will go in after school or during weekends to mow the lawn

two or three times a week. You could arrange to do the watering, too.

If you've got a family lawn and know about gardening and fertilizing, it might impress your customers if you inform them that you have just sprinkled such-and-such a fertilizer on your lawn. If theirs is a deprived, scruffy wilderness, they might take your hint and then your season's work will show rather better results.

But check the equipment they expect you to use. Is the mower recently sharpened, or a trifle rusty so that the most energetic pushing leaves the stronger stalks still standing? And are the blades set correctly, so that you are giving their greensward a good trim, but not shaving it near bald? And what about the trimming shears? Have they been oiled and sharpened? No matter how eager you may be, you can't do a decent job if the tools are inadequate. So if you find they are, ask that they should be sharpened and oiled, or offer – for an extra charge, needless to say – to arrange for it to be done yourself. Maybe, with the help of your Mum or Dad, you can manage the shears yourself, but you'll probably have to organize for the local gardening centre or hardware store to collect the mower, sharpen it and return it in time for the first cutting. Meanwhile, if the lawn is in a terrible state, you can offer to do some rough cutting, raking and fertilizing.

If you have some new neighbours moving in with a garden that looks more like a rubbish dump, ask if they are planning a lawn. If so, would they like you to help prepare the ground and lay the turf?

They will probably be so busy painting and furnishing that they will be only too pleased for you to take over. Ask advice from any gardening experts you know. They will tell you that the most important thing is to prepare the ground properly first, which will probably involve lots of digging, and clearing out builders' debris and other litter, then some heavy forking and raking over.

But when, a couple of months later, your spare-time boss can boast the best outdoors green carpet in the neighbourhood, and you've bought a super new fishing rod with your earnings, won't it be worthwhile!

L3 LEAFLET AND POSTER DESIGNER

Creative? Good at lettering? If you enjoy drawing (especially cartooning) and writing your own magazines, why not put your talents to valuable use? Approach some local shops and businesses and ask them if they would like you to design and produce an illustrated leaflet for them, advertising their goods or services. If your father is a printer or your mother has the use of a duplicating machine in her office, you're well away.

First of all, design a 'dummy' show-off leaflet for an imaginary business. Make it eye-catching. Add some quirky humour – try to outdo the telly-ad jokers!

L4 LEAF RAKER

Another gardening job for a junior, energetic person who wants some savings for Christmas.

If you spot anyone in your locality with leaf-ridden lawns, knock on the door and offer to clear their grass.

If you happen to have one of those efficient quarter-circle wire rakes at home, and your parents don't mind you using it in the cause of earning pocket-money, take it along with you. Perhaps you could offer some hints on how important it is to get the dead leaves off if your employers want their grass to flourish, and even (after seeking advice) suggest which fertilizer you could sprinkle on ready for the spring sowing.

L5 LIBRARY HELPER

A lot of public libraries get desperately short-staffed during holiday periods, and might welcome you for a couple of hours' standing-in several times a week during peak time.

You will have to learn how to check books in and out, return them to their proper places on the shelves, and answer queries.

It makes a great deal of difference if you enjoy reading yourself, too. You could recall a Sir Walter Scott title for a forgetful old lady who is looking for an historical romance, or you might suggest one of Roald Dahl's hilarious fantasies for a small boy who keeps dithering round the bookshelves, unable to make up his mind, while his mother just stands nagging in the background.

L6 LOOKING AFTER SMALL CHILDREN WHILE MUM OR DAD IS OUT

This is *not* child-minding, because in order to be a recognized childminder you have to register with the local council. This is just helping out for anything from a half-hour to a morning or afternoon, when a mother or father with young children wants somebody reliable to keep them fed and amused while they go out.

I know plenty of parents who find that if they need

somebody to look after the kids while they go shopping, to the dentist or doctor, for instance, it is far cheaper and more reliable to ask the friendly, understanding, trustworthy girl up the road than invest in a costly au pair (even if they had the room), or haul squalling under-fives with them everywhere.

Try asking a few local families. They will be far more confident if you can tell them that you have done this kind of looking-after before, if you have younger brothers and sisters or infant relations for whom you baby-sit.

Ask what they usually do with their children during the time they will be leaving them with you. If they seem a bit uninspired, ask if you can get them finger-painting or making cakes – depending upon their age, of course. Don't be too ambitious, because lots of little girls and boys who seem like angels when you are interviewed by their parents can turn into devils the moment Mum and Dad close the front door behind them. It's far better to have them think you a meanie than to have to call the doctor or the police!

This brings us to that most important point: insist on a list of places the parents will be while you are looking after their children: office numbers, and even a vague itinerary of shops if they have gone shopping. Also the names, addresses and phone numbers of one or more close friends, the family doctor and the local police station (you should know this, anyway).

And, though you may have an inborn genius for communicating with small children, don't let your pride at doing a job well show too much. Some time before mother or father is due back, start preparing the kids for the pleasure – maybe the picture will be for Daddy, because he has had such a hard day driving down the motorway; maybe the cakes will be for Mummy, because she probably didn't have time to eat, dashing around the office.

All loving parents have twinges of guilt about leaving tiny ones, especially if sobbing on the doorstep while they run for the bus. It will make them eternally grateful to you that you don't hog the babies for your own pleasure, but think of them as well, and they will think of you first when the next crisis arises.

Charge the going baby-sitting fees. You might deserve more, but you could price yourself out of work.

M1 MAGICIAN (OR CONJUROR OR FORTUNE-TELLER)

Got any good tricks up your sleeve? If you're a bit of a novice, but have the motivation, get several how-to-make-magic books from your library and put in some practice: illusions, spoofs, mystifying scientific experiments, card tricks, disappearing tricks, sleight-of-hand acts. My favourite handbook for starting you off is *How to Make Magic* (Studio Vista, £1.25).

Make – perhaps with Mum and Dad's help – your magician's costume: top hat made from painted cardboard, swirling black cloak with red satin lining made from curtain material or remnants, bamboo wand filched from the garden shed. Add false moustache and eyebrows plus an infectious, tricky smile!

Once you feel ready to fool and win over a small audience, prepare a few leaflets advertising your services, preferably coloured and illustrated – something like this: 'Want some real magic to brighten up your Christmas or birthday party? Riveting entertainment, bound to bring fun and laughs for your guests. Different age-groups specially catered for. Small prizes arranged if desired. Please contact Dan Jones who will be pleased to come round for a consultation at your convenience.' Then follows your address and phone number plus what you think is the going rate for performance fees. (Or write 'Fees to be arranged'.)

Fortune-telling is specially popular with girls, since it involves lots of dressing up, acting expertise and some cunning preparation beforehand.

Organize a dim corner of the room, with dark-curtained backdrop and a small table covered with a black cloth. Cover these with silver foil star and moon shapes. On the table place your crystal ball, with candles either side. The ball need not be the real thing –

just a small goldfish bowl placed upside down and glue-covered with silver sparkle, or an ordinary light bulb, balanced on a toilet roll holder, again sparkle-glued.

Fortune-tellers' costumes should be exotic and gypsy-like – borrowed caftan, headdress with bandeau stitched with curtain rings, and lots of beads and bracelets. Not forgetting eye-black, purple lipstick and blusher.

The fortunes you tell? The secret is to swot up on anything you can discover about your audience, which they think you wouldn't know. Anything – a pet they are especially fond of, a birthday present soon to be given, a secret hobby – and weave your predictions around them. Suppose a friend spotted a small guest picking flowers from a neighbour's garden – a small hint that this crime was widely observed can give them a harmless scare that will have you viewed with astonished respect – and leave the neighbour's marigolds uninvaded.

M2 MAKING TEA

If you aren't too snooty to take on a menial task like this and do it well, you can learn more about work and life than you dreamt you would.

What kind of organization are you interested in? A newspaper office, building contractor, bank, dress shop, architect's drawing office, estate agent's, art gallery, television studio, theatre . . .? Well, look about, and in any big town or city, with a bit of trying, you are bound to find a niche where a willing boy or girl (especially those who keep pestering politely) could get a half-day Saturday or holiday job. You might decide whether or not to make your career there, depending on what you observe.

Is the firm too sloppily run? Couldn't you do better yourself? You may well go home and say that to your Mum, but could you actually detail your criticisms and offer some really feasible, constructive ideas that would help make the business more fruitful? Opportunities may open up if you are always keen to help out wherever you can.

Lots of people started as teaboys or teagirls. They got on because they did their job well and knew how to listen.

Lots of bosses, you will find, given a really good cup of tea or steaming hot coffee, exactly as ordered, will relax and talk. They might reveal secrets and wisdoms to you that they would not share with their co-directors. If you want to get where they have got, listen.

But, needless to say, present them with their beverage at its best. If you are working in an office with, say, seven executives to cater for, memorize or note down their preferences, Tea, well-brewed, two lumps of sugar, one digestive biscuit for Mr Brown. Cona coffee, no milk, one saccharine for Mrs Johnson, his co-manager. Hot chocolate for his secretary. An offer of a glass of water for the liver salts which sales manager Mr Robertson keeps in his desk drawer instead of teatime tea. That herb tea concoction for the model-girls who have been posing in the studio, which you have ready brewing even before they have asked for it, because you know when the session is due to end.

Tea-making can get you anywhere, so long as you let it brew properly!

M3 MARKET STALL HELPER

Here's a job that requires you to be quick on the uptake, not to say a bit cunning!

You may know a relative who can teach you the tricks of stall marketing – otherwise you are going to have to learn the kind of verbal expertise that may not get you A-levels but calls for just as much hard work and intelligence.

People like to be cheered up and have their wits sharpened when they have to pay out for potatoes, onions, carrots, dresses or saucepans. Make a joke about it. If you're bright enough, key it to the latest news: one of those exaggerated headlines about the spread of some kind of onion disease or the shortage of cotton maybe!

In a market, everybody loves to battle verbally. Tease shoppers a bit and sharpen their wits with a few sallies.

People don't get enough compliments nowadays, and if you spot a middle-aged lady looking a bit down, quickly sort out the nicest remark you can make about her – her blue eyes, whatever she's wearing, the way she knows how to choose a really fresh vegetable or a bargain-price style – and tell her so. You are not just making yourself a regular customer – you are jollying up somebody who may be feeling really depressed and giving them a lift for the whole day.

But any good old-fashioned market stallholder will tell you that brightening a doleful face with a smile and a cheerful comment will persuade people to come and buy from you every Saturday morning instead of queuing up at the impersonal supermarket. And, provided you don't agree to give the over-ripe tomatoes or the flawed towels to the notoriously short-sighted pensioners of the neighbourhood, this can be both a moral and a happy way of earning a spare-time living.

M4 MENDING, HEMMING AND ALTERING

Not much in demand, until times get tight, and people cannot afford to replace clothes in need of repair.

A job for the very painstaking young person. Repairing a hole in a costly and treasured jersey, perhaps. Letting down or raising the hem of one of those dresses that is the bulwark of a neighbour's wardrobe, but is getting too long or too short. Stitching up the usual come-apart seams on so many cheap children's and adults' clothes. Maybe altering skirts and jeans from an older child for the younger one in the family. These are all time-consuming tasks many grown-ups would be grateful to pay for, when they arrive home with just enough energy to cook the supper, put the kids to bed, then flop out.

M5 MESSENGER BOY OR GIRL

You might get a job like this in a big hotel when the regular messenger is away. Have you got a cousin in the job, or an uncle who is a commissionaire, .who might recommend you?

This job involves a lot of running around, and being polite to people who may be rather tired and not very polite to you. But, as a famous newspaper editor once said, locked up in prison for espionage on what he thought was a perfectly straightforward interview and a nice trip abroad: 'You should look upon everything in life as a first-class experience.'

Flatter people, cheer them up when they are slumped down with jet lag, and try very hard to put names to faces. It's not a bad idea to check with the booking desk who is likely to come in, and then think what films they have made, what races they have driven in, or how they won the bronze medal in the Olympics. Then write everything they say down in your diary. Then, not only will you be making some money for the time being, but you will have some interesting anecdotes for the future, too.

But, needless to say, always be discreet. Just offer praise, and never question. Never presume that the man with the film actress is her husband! You'll gain a heftier tip by being meticulously efficient and offering a few selected compliments.

M6 MILKMAN'S RUNNER

Busy holiday times and Saturday mornings are your cue to chase after your local milk float, which may very well need another pair of hands, when demands

for the usual pinta-a-day are quadrupled. You should be nimble on your feet (try counting the steps and stairs in a heat wave or snow storm) and no butter fingers! This is a worthwhile job that can make you some useful friends if you are cheerful and obliging. There is nothing like being remembered as someone who came up on time with the wherewithal for the morning cuppa, and it might just lead to another job.

O1 OUTDOORS CLEANING

You don't mind the rain, wind or cold? It doesn't bother you if your hands get a bit rough, when you're earning money for something you really need?

Lots of grown-ups, spoiled by central heating or maybe very busy, are looking out for a young person to wash or scrape down the outsides of their house or flat.

P1 PAGE BOY OR GIRL (*see also* HOTEL CHAMBERMAID OR BOOTBOY; MESSENGER)

Some hotels may need a youngster to help carry bags, page guests for telephone calls or visitors, or call taxis during the tourist high season.

This job may not be well paid, but if you're cheery, polite and demonstratively eager to please, you may do well out of tips. For instance, if, when you carry a suitcase for a holidaymaker into her bedroom, you chat about the local beauty spot, ancient abbey or fishing loch worth visiting, she might reward you with double the amount she was thinking of giving you.

P2 PARENT HELPER

Working for your parents can be a very tricky business, because obviously you will not have the usual relationship between employer and employee.

Some rather silly, spoiling mothers and fathers will pay for almost any job you do about the house. This will not teach you the value of money or stand you in good stead in adult life – many a marriage has gone on the rocks because a pampered husband or wife, subconsciously at least, sees every household task as requiring some kind of financial reward.

Every young person should expect to do their share of the chores for free, and you can only expect to be paid for some special arduous job like repainting the living-room, for instance, or recementing the sun terrace.

Of course, it may be different if you are being given a job as filing clerk in your father's office or as a presser in your Mum's dress shop, so long as you are treated with neither more nor less consideration and discipline than any of the other employees.

The same sometimes applies to uncles, aunts and grandparents, especially if they happen to be very close and fond of you. Don't take advantage of a doting widowed Granny if she offers you double the going cost for putting up some shelves for her when you know she is hard up.

Naturally, you cannot afford to turn down job offers from parents or close relatives if you're desperate for some extra money. But, given the choice, won't you get more adventure and sense of achievement from working for a stranger?

P3 PARTY WARDEN (OR ENTERTAINER)

Many a parental heart sinks at the thought of giving the obligatory birthday party for a small son or daughter. All the squeals and squalls, the fights and the tears, the spills and mess, and the inevitable small child who is sick all over the sofa.

This is where you could be a godsend – helping to prepare the goodies, then, when the guests arrive, tying bibs on the littlest ones and seeing that they are led to the lavatory before there's a puddle on the carpet. You will be helping to see that every child gets what he or she wants to eat, scraping jelly spills off the floor, or even diplomatically preventing two horrible little boys from embarking upon a chocolate blancmange war and splattering the hosts' precious wallpaper!

Also offer to help at adult parties. Most hosts love going to other people's parties, but hate giving their own, because they get into such a flap, trying to fix their hair and the soufflé at the same time. They could appreciate somebody prepared to do some of the hard work, like table-laying and washing-up. Offer to act as a waiter or waitress, taking coats, handing round drinks, and emptying ash trays. If you are a good cook, maybe you could make some of the dishes.

Ask what you would be expected to wear. If you are just going to spend your time over the kitchen sink, up to your elbows in detergent, it doesn't matter if you come in your scruffiest jeans. But if you are to be circulating among the guests, then choose something neat and discreet from your wardrobe and ask if this would be suitable. On no account turn up in some ravishing shirt and skin-tight white jeans, upstaging your paunchy, grey flannel-suited host, or in a gorgeous see-through long dress that outshines his wife's dowdy blue brocade. They won't ask *you* round again, however efficient you may have been! Try to be smiling and relaxed, but not sloppy.

But if both the hosts and their guests are impressed by the unobtrusive, willing way you help to take the strain out of entertaining, they will probably call upon you whenever another party comes up in their social circle.

If you know any very well-heeled party-givers, you might get together with a friend and offer your services as a couple.

P4 PENSIONER WATCHPERSON

Have you got a soft spot for old people? Are you the sort of boy or girl who is especially conscientious, patient, observant and caring?

Look around and you'll find a lot of pensioners in your neighbourhood, many housebound or bed-ridden, who have a real need for somebody like you to take messages, run errands and, most important of all, check regularly that they are all right. Maybe they can't afford your services, but relatives who are busy working or who have heavy family responsibilities might be only too glad to pay someone to check up for them. Often, an overworked young mum will be only too relieved for a young neighbour who is not too emotionally involved to pop round every day to listen to Grandma's stream of petty demands and complaints.

P5 PET MINDER (*see also* CAT-CARING; DOG-WALKING; FISH-FEEDING)

It's worth spending some time assessing your possibilities for earning by looking after all kinds of pets – not just cats and dogs, but rabbits, guinea-pigs, hamsters, budgerigars . . . Lots of people go away for odd weekends as well as their holidays. Some childless working couples may need to call upon you when they both have to go away on business at the same time. If you are reliable and animal-loving, you could build up a steady stream of work all the year round, especially if you advertise yourself. Put cards in several of the local newsagents, and ask any neighbours with pets.

When you call for interviews, tell your prospective

employers what pets, if any, you have. If they are the kind of people who clearly treat their spaniel or Siamese as if it were a baby, make a point of showing how affectionate you can be, too – they will be more likely to choose you as their pet-minder if there are rivals for the job.

When making arrangements with them before they go away, always write down feeding-times and diet carefully. Make sure you have their holiday or working address and phone number. Also the name and phone number of their vet, in case of illness or accident. Unless you are taking their pet into your own home, you will need a key to their house, of course. If they do not know you personally, it would be a good idea to get a reference from your parents or teacher, confirming your honesty and reliability, not only with pet-feeding, but with locking up as well.

P6 PET SHOP DOGSBODY

If you love animals and have a way with them, this is just the job for you. You will get enormous pleasure handling and caring for small creatures, especially if you happen to live in a flat, where it is not possible to keep a pet if you have any regard for their needs and freedoms.

The relationship between man and animal (or fish, or reptile!) is something very special, and not everybody is good at this. But maybe you have the gift – you know how to be gentle and you never forget how and when the animals need to be fed. And if you have ambitions to be a veterinary surgeon, it can be well worth your while in more ways than one to offer your services for a few hours a week.

It is hard, smelly work cleaning out cages and swabbing down the floors and counters. But if you are fond of the guinea-pig or parrot you are charring for – well, it's not such a chore, is it?

If you are working in a pet boarding kennels or cattery, be especially careful about washing your hands in disinfected water between handling animals. In these situations, too-much-travelled, upset creatures all too easily contract diseases or infections and pass them on.

Always check, too, that cages and hutches are properly secured after feeding. My local pet shop is next door to the off-licence, whose manager is rather over-fond of whisky. A nephew of the pet shop owner was a bit careless about locking up at Saturday closing-time, and a couple of hours later the manager happened to look down from the wine shelves to see a large green snake sliding under the back door. The shock made him teetotal for nearly a week! And one embarrassed nephew got the sack!

P7 PHOTOGRAPHER'S ASSISTANT

Do you enjoy taking snaps? Maybe you'd like to earn enough to set up your own darkroom.

There are two kinds of job you can look out for. First, spare-time assistant to a family photographer. You know the kind: a one-person business, probably with a little shop, doing local weddings, christenings and family portraits. Go through the phone book and ring or call on all the ones you can find within a reasonable distance of your home and ask if they want help.

Even if you know nothing about cameras or developing film, you can show willing to learn. Before going for an interview, read up any books on photography you can find in the local library, or quiz any camera-mad friends.

The second kind of job would be helping a freelance press photographer. If you have ambitions to take up journalism, this would give you plenty of experience. It is not half as exciting or glamorous as it sounds when you have spent two hours on some chilly, rain-swept doorstep, waiting for some boring old councillor to return from a committee meeting. Especially as your job will be to carry all the bags and set up the tripods. Sometimes it can be harrowing, but occasionally you might be lucky, if some famous star, pop singer, poet or footballer happens to be filming or holidaying in the locality.

P8 PORTRAIT ARTIST

If you are talented – whether it's with pen, crayons, chalks, water-colours, poster paints or oils – this could develop into quite a profitable sideline.

Quite a lot of close families like the idea of having a portrait of a relative. If you suggested it, an old lady might commission a chalk drawing of her beloved baby grandson.

Yes, I know sketches and paintings have been largely overtaken by photographs. But there are still many who would prefer to have the former hanging on their living-room wall.

First, needless to say, you need the special talent for producing a likeness and capturing your sitter's personality. Some designers and painters may be brilliant at landscapes and abstracts, but are hopeless at people.

How do you go about getting commissions? First, prepare your folio: get together some portraits of your family and friends, preferably those your would-be clients would know and recognize. Most popular commissions, you'll find, will be for children. So get in some practice.

And, don't forget, your portraits need not be confined to human beings. Many a pet-lover would like a portrait of an adored old labrador or tabby. Horses? Well, if you've frequently sketched them, you could have a try, but you'd need to be a really excellent artist as well as experienced. Try a semi-profile over the stable door. Make your fee very small. You can always raise the prices as your popularity spreads.

Then, once you've got your commission, it helps if your sitters are willing for you to do a few rough preliminary sketches as they sit about reading, playing, knitting, or cuddling a child or pet. In this way you can make your portrait especially meaningful, because you will be able to capture a mannerism everybody sees as familiar. 'Oh, yes, Gran's always sitting with her glasses on the top of her head like that, with old Ginger in her lap,' they'll say, and find the likeness twice as good as it really is! Or: 'Baby John always sleeps on his back with one arm up on the pillow like that, doesn't he? Just like him!' Otherwise, your portrait could have resembled half the babies on the estate!

P9 POTATO LIFTING

Another seasonal job for a youngster with plenty of muscle who enjoys hard physical work. There is also lifting other root crops, like beet, turnips or swedes, for small farmers or smallholders who don't find it worth while to harvest them mechanically.

You may find you'll be paid by the hundredweight of potatoes you dig up – it's an incentive!

P10 POTTER

If you are good at pottery at school, why not make use of your abilities by making gifts – personalized napkin rings, egg cups, casserole dishes, ashtrays, candle holders or ornamental animals? You can probably think up a score more ideas.

What about equipment for baking and glazing? You might be able to make use of your school's kiln. Or enrol for night classes at your local adult education institute.

Check the going prices of pottery in your neighbourhood gift shops, and make yours considerably lower. Unless you are really brilliant, you cannot expect your work to be up to that of experienced professionals.

R1 REPAIRING AND REPAINTING TOYS

Most families pass down toys from one child to another. Most toys get bashed about and chipped and, though still just as sturdy and with all the play potential, won't be received by a younger brother or sister unless refurbished. First, check what is to be done. Is it safe and in working order? Oil any parts that may need oiling. Do tyres need to be renewed? Screws tightened or replaced? If it is a kid's bicycle, does the chain need tightening or replacing?

If you are simply repainting a child's wooden or metal toy that is obviously still quite sturdy, but looking rather battered and used, this how to do it: sandpaper it down first (use rough sandpaper), then wipe with a damp cloth. You don't have to sandpaper all thc paint off – just enough to make a clean job of it. Go over it again with a finer-grain sandpaper. Finally, wipe with a damp cloth to get rid of all the dust, and you are ready to paint.

Take your time on this. You probably want to get the job done quickly, and present it to your customers. But paint, especially the best paint, needs time to dry. And, if you do the second coat too soon, it wrinkles and you'll have to start all over again. So why not put on an undercoat one afternoon or evening before you are going out or watching a special programme on television, giving it lots of time to dry properly? Then add the top coat the next day. Perhaps, if your customers agree (which they should), give it a second coat. Some may even suggest a third. But leave plenty of time between paintings, putting the toy on newspaper in your bedroom or the toolshed, where there is no dust or people to brush by it, and the finished product will look much smoother and shinier, and even quite sharp bumpings won't make it chip. If you are buying the paint to repair a plaything or bike for others, don't just ask for the name you last heard mentioned on a television ad. Either buy the make your customer asks for, or else ask the advice of your local friendly handyman. Some paints are much more batter-proof than others. And don't forget, when buying on behalf of others, keep the receipt!

R2 RESTAURANT (OR EATING-PLACE) FACTOTUM

Restaurants, tearooms, sandwich, chicken, hamburger and fish and chip bars, and roadside cafes are often desperate for an extra pair of hands, especially during busy times. This could be the pre-Christmas going-out season, holiday-time, or the high season for fishing if you live near some well-stocked rivers, lochs or reservoirs. It could be that a factory or a motorway is being built in your neighbourhood and there are hundreds of hungry men queuing up for snacks and meals.

Make a list of the likely local places, then go round and call on the manager – or boss – starting with the ones you'd prefer to work in. A tidy, shy, well-mannered girl might prefer to put on a neat waitress uniform and work in the kind of quiet restaurant or Ye Olde Tea Shoppe that is favoured by retired gentlefolk ordering scones, strawberries and cream, with tea properly brewed in one of those old-fashioned pots; or where young lovers and wedding anniversary celebrators whisper discreetly over some *bœuf bourguignon* with a bottle of Beaujolais. A tough lad who is saving up for a tent and some hill-climbing equipment for his cycling holidays in the Alps might be happy slapping out ham butties and egg and chips in the rough and rowdy atmosphere of a lorrydriver's pull-up in his usual old, patched jeans. (Well, the second oldest, then.)

Make sure you know exactly what work is expected of you – it could be taking the orders, laying tables, and arranging flowers. Or it could be all day every day in some tiny hell-hole of a kitchen scouring greasy pans or cleaning lavatories and dustbins, whether the sign reads 'La Terrine du chef' or 'Joe's Place'.

Watch out that you aren't underpaid – catering bosses are notoriously mean. And expect decent meals free with the job – not congealing leftovers and scrapings.

Be meticulous about washing your hands between duties. Well, you wouldn't like to think that you might end up with food poisoning if you were eating out, would you?

Cheerful, brisk service will gain you bigger tips. If you moon about by the service door daydreaming about your favourite pop star or new shoes to be bought next Saturday, while ignored customers become increasingly impatient, you'll be lucky to get one at all.

Incidentally, if you happen to notice that there are mice or bugs in the kitchen, and that the organization is dangerously unhygienic – if you uncover rotting refuse within feet of fresh meat, or see food that is definitely 'off' still on the menu – be a good citizen and report this to the local health inspector. You can make it anonymous.

R3 RUBBISH SHIFTER

In this throwaway age, there is often too much litter around. Many householders – especially those newly moved-in, with lots of building debris, junk and packaging to get rid of – won't mind your offer to clear their rubbish away for them.

Just look round your neighbourhood for those with rubbish piled in the garden and ask anybody you know who happens to be struggling with do-it-yourself renovating.

This job usually entails piling rubbish up ready for

the skip or local garbage van to take away, and perhaps burning some. It's a mucky job, for which you are entitled to ask as much as for baby-sitting, since you have, possibly, to put up with cut hands and torn clothes.

There is one bonus – you might discover, among what other people consider worthless, quite a few treasures. A ten-year-old boy I know came upon a vintage 1950 comic among a pile of old newspapers he was supposed to put on a bonfire, plus a ninety-year-old marble and doll, which he sold and which paid for a new football kit.

S1 SALES TICKET WRITER

Got a nice sense of humour? Quick off the mark with a smart phrase? Good at cartooning? Then offer to design, write and illustrate sales tickets for local shops and stalls. All you need are some white cards – plain postcards or large sheets from your local art shop cut up – and some fat, colourful felt pens.

First, go round likely employers with a good sample of your work. Key it, if you can, to the local news or the national headlines. Suppose there is an international debate on the world shortage of cotton – wouldn't it be a good idea to approach the local fabric shop with some cards saying, perhaps, *Cottoning on? We've still got some left!?* The cornier the better – it makes people laugh! Then, having discovered what colours and amounts of cotton fabrics they have (simply by asking at the counter), illustrate your cards with any available patterns and approach the manager with your cards. He or she should be agreeably surprised. I'm sure you can think up loads of better slogans about anything from tomatoes to tinned catfood. Once they've accepted the idea and are willing to take a regular supply, make sure you have a proper written contract – say, twenty a week for a month, renewable.

S2 'SECURITY GUARD'

No, you don't have to be one of those fierce-looking toughies with a crash helmet and a Dobermann pinscher on a lead to keep an eye on somebody's house while they are on holiday. Just be observant and use your common sense. Look after their house with care and thought.

Don't pop in at regular times to see that everything is O K – any would-be burglar could check by watching you for a couple of days. If your arrangement is to observe just once a day, try to vary your times.

If it is holiday-time, especially, suggest to your employers that you drop in occasionally for several hours – watching television, lazing in the garden, or reading a book. Perhaps you could enjoy a bit of peace and quiet that you don't get at home.

Show that the place is occupied by leaving different lights switched on – the landing light one visit, the bedroom the next. This won't stop any professional burglar, but it could deter silly juveniles.

If you notice a window-catch broken, a door-lock scraped, a drawer opened or possessions missing, you should phone the police immediately and notify the neighbours. Check with the householders, too, whether water and central heating will be turned off and what to do if there are any problems.

If people are willing for you to use their place while they are away, don't abuse the agreement. Just to put it one way: if it was your own off-white carpet, would you spill coffee all over it?

It doesn't take long in a neighbourhood for people to realize who is trustworthy enough for this kind of job. If you have coped with a couple of security guard jobs during the spring holidays, for example, and the families have come back relieved to find the place not just as it was when they left it, but even tidier – you're on! And, when you find yourself too busy, you could always recommend a younger brother, sister or friend to take over.

S3 SHAMPOOER
(*see also* **HOME HAIRDRESSER**)

Well, look what happened to Greta Garbo and Twiggy! They both started off in the local hairdressing salon as

lather girls. I used to find this difficult to understand since it seemed to me, when I was fifteen, desperate for prospects and the wherewithal to buy some shoes, that all the job involved was sticking a strange head into a basin filled with froth, so your customers barely got a glimpse of you, anyway.

Of course, I was wrong. Personality, as well as efficiency, really does count here. Customers need you – otherwise, why wouldn't they be doing their own hair at home? Half your work is cut out categorizing your client – the bored, well-heeled neurotic lady or gent wishing for a chat they can get cheaper from you than from their unfriendly neighbourhood psychiatrist, or the busy man or woman who just wants a fast wash, set and blow-dry and no trivial remarks about weather or politics while thinking out a business report; maybe that in-between person – the one who, like all of us at some time or another, just wants to look different, but can't decide on a new hair-style, let alone the correct shampoo or rinse.

Here's where you come in. Without stepping on the boss's toes, try suggesting to Mrs Brown as tactfully as possible that she change her arid, over-tinted bee-hive (for which the salon charges more) to a simple grey fringe with her rather fine hair curling gently round her ears. Hopefully, she'll come back to you, and the salon will benefit rather than losing by trying to gain an easy profit.

Tell Mrs Smith, whose interminable de-frizzing has been costing her a bomb every fortnight, that it suits her lovely face to leave her hair as it is, just reshaped and tweaked out.

Even if you don't want to become a hair stylist, this is, as you can see, a good way of meeting people. Want to become a lawyer's clerk? An editor's secretary? A television presenter? Look up the list of customers for the day, ask the receptionist who is who and use your initiative – that's what Greta Garbo and Twiggy did!

On the other hand, you might genuinely want to make hairdressing a career, knowing that looking after people's tops is an art. So watch and learn – that's what Vidal Sassoon did, and it took him from London's East End all over the world.

As for pay, check with local hairdressing salons or ask any shampooer friends. The more fashionable salons, like horse stables, are likely to offer less. But that's your choice.

S4 SHOP ASSISTANT OR SHELVER

Loads of opportunities here. If you have the urge to run a selling-place yourself, this is the way to learn.

Oddly enough, though some of your teachers may consider you daft, and your end-of-term reports always read something like 'Never tries', I know lots of kids who make a really good job of counter assistant in the local supermarket. It might be something to do with operating on your own initiative.

You may be employed unpacking and stocking shelves. You may be a counter assistant. Elbow grease and conscientiousness bring quick rewards, because shop assistant in some neighbourhoods is mistakenly considered to be an in-between job and not worth doing properly.

You can get a lot of fun and pleasure out of serving over a counter. You'll enjoy chatting to people (maybe your Mum and Dad are too exhausted to talk to you in the evenings when you feel like going into problems), helping old ones who can't add up and distraught young mothers with a baby squalling alongside just as they are trying to balance the housekeeping.

And, if you really think you could be a supermarket manager or run a shop, why not show how, with some constructive ideas? If there was a sudden potato, pea, chocolate or ice-cream shortage, what would you do? Secrete them in a back shelf at double the price? Or put them out front, cheaper than down the road? Work that one out!

S5 SINGING CAROLS

Sounds a bit silly to some kids, but for many older

people it brings enormous pleasure to hear young voices outside the window on a wintry night, giving far more warmth, in a way, than any central heating can.

Some carollers spoil it for everybody by yelling out an off-key, obscure version of *Good King Wenceslas* for thirty seconds flat, then bashing on the door and holding out an empty palm. That's cheating.

Go round first of all to those you happen to know have money to spare. Christmas party hosts could hire you to give their guests a rousing seasonal welcome. But when sentimental old ladies and gentlemen offer you next day's grocery money because they are so pleased to see a happy young face, forget your profits and accept only token payment. Never, however, do it for free – you will injure old people's pride, because they used to work for a living too.

S6 SNOW CLEARING

Not what you'd call a regular job, unless you happen to live in the kind of countryside where seasonal snow-falls can be expected, in which case you're on to a good thing. Make arrangements before the skies turn grey. Collect salt, spades and all the necessaries. Keep your ears open for the weather forecasts, and be on the spot first thing in the morning, so the boss can saunter rather than slide down the front step, because you have cleared it and sprinkled it with salt an hour before. Helping out at local farms if you live in the countryside can save the lives of many animals and earn you gratitude as well as money.

If jobs in your area are hard to get around wintertime, it is common sense and responsible to suggest to elderly people (and those with prams and babies) that slipping on icy steps and breaking a wrist or an ankle could be avoided if they were swept and sprinkled in freezing weather.

But be fair – charge only what you think they can afford. If you can extract as much as possible out of the mean old curmudgeon with a vast house and plenty in the bank – well, good for you. But wouldn't sweeping the drifts off some deprived old widow's front path for next to nothing give you a nice warm feeling too?

S7 STABLE HAND

Horse crazy? Pony crackers? Donkey mad? Some people are scared to bits by the sight of clomping hooves, and cannot bear the stink of a healthy pile of steaming manure. Some boys and girls get enormous pleasure working at clearing soiled straw, rubbing down, and mixing the bran suppers at the local riding school, holiday centre or farm.

The chances are that you'll get paid very little for this kind of job, because it is what used to be known as a 'dedicated occupation'. In other words, the employers know that you would be happy to do it for nothing, so they will pay you peanuts. And, of course, most young people – especially town- and city-dwellers – find being a stable help a lot more rewarding than working on a factory-line. Think about it, then work out your priorities. If you think that you are being given a very rough deal financially, why not organize a get-together with the other stable helpers and your more senior colleagues and talk it out? Find out the name of the rival stable, perhaps, and ask them what the going wage is.

S8 SWEEPER-UP

No matter if your mother tells you you're an incompetent layabout, your father says you were born useless, and, somehow, everybody else seems to get the best-paid jobs. It's often the simple, humble, common or garden job like sweeping up that could end up with you having more savings in the bank than the rest of your class. And anyway, you can think your own thoughts at the same time, can't you?

Offer to sweep up for any neighbours, inside or out. Lots of stallkeepers, offices or shops could do with a sweeper-up after closing time.

T1 TALENT CONTEST TACKLER

This is a one-off job, as they say. It may be treated as a joke, but you never know your potential. And even if you lose, you will have had a worthwhile experience and will have lots of amusing stories to tell your friends.

Make sure you've got a good snap of yourself. Think three times about the way you word your letter or fill in the form. Will they think it worth while looking twice at your entry if you say your ambition is to be a footballer or woman prime minister, true though this may be?

Talent competitions are for young people who can gain interest and attention by doing something well or thinking up something original or with extra style, whether it's singing, dancing, joking, cartooning or even fishing. Not to mention magic, acrobatics or imitations.

Television studios and big manufacturers offer their competitions in order to attract new talent. So do holiday camps, where so-called 'star managers' and agents are always ready to seek out the young ones before anybody else.

So do your best, in your own way – whether it's filling in the form or just jumping on the platform at two seconds' notice at the holiday resort. But be sure to consult your parents before signing anything.

T2 THEATRE BACKSTAGER

This sort of job is much sought after, because it offers so many opportunities to anybody with artistic leanings. If you are drawn to the lights, the thrill and the drama of the stage, this can lead you in all kinds of directions.

It may not offer much more, but even if you are working away for next to nothing, you can be learning more than they ever taught you at school about the theatre.

You might be asked to make tea, fetch and carry, or iron costumes; perhaps you'll have to call the actors when it's their time to go on stage, or even help fix the lights, paint the scenery, and help with make-up.

You will soon realize how much hard work and patience goes into putting on a show – the hours spent trying on costumes, making-up, and arranging the lighting. Whether or not your ambition is to be a dresser, a stage manager, member of the chorus or the star, a few weeks helping out during holiday-time could make up your mind.

Look in your local papers, and apply to every local theatre or theatre club. It's probably best to call at the stage door when you know the boss will not be too busy. You are bound to be turned away if you knock on the door half an hour before the play is due to begin.

Everybody in the theatre likes a bit of flattery, so go and see the show if you can or at least get a programme so that you know the names of the cast as well as those behind the scenes, and especially the producer.

T3 TYPING

Have your parents bought you a typewriter for Christmas? Are you learning to type at school? This is the kind of spare-time job that can earn you a very healthy income, provided your speeds and accuracy are good.

Look through the local papers and ask around, because you might find a local author or retired professor who would like manuscripts typed, or small businesses who do not normally employ a full-time typist.

Ask any friends you know who do this how much

they charge and check the local advertisements. If your work is good and fast, do not accept less than the going payment.

If you're really enterprising, and haven't learned shorthand at school, spend your savings on a brief course. You'd be surprised how fast you can learn during the Easter holidays in order to earn your wardrobe money in August. Or start learning during the winter and work in the spring holidays and weekends, for a well-heeled holiday in the summer.

U1 UPHOLSTERY CLEANER

This is a job that most people hate to have to do, so since it is both difficult and costly to find professionals, here's a chance for you to step in for a price.

Get the employers to supply (or at least choose) the cleaning materials, and, checking with them, follow the instructions to the letter. That way, if their low-quality fabric shrinks or fades, they cannot blame you.

As this often turns out to be a much tougher, longer job than it looks at first glance, I would suggest to them that you are paid by the hour.

V1 VEGETABLE GROWER

If you are lucky enough to have lots of growing space round your home, you could ask your parents if they would allow you to start up your own small market garden. Anybody who has had carrots, broccoli, lettuce and beans picked and eaten within minutes knows how delicious they are compared with the plastic-packed variety you get in the supermarket.

Enlist the advice of any local gardening enthusiasts you know, and work out what sort of vegetables are mostly in demand before deciding what to grow. If you deliver them yourself, arranged attractively in one of those big cane market baskets, you'll have plenty of customers willing to pay the going price. Consider setting up a roadside stall or placing cards in local shop windows.

V2 VET'S ASSISTANT

A joy for anybody who loves animals and has ambitions to become a veterinary surgeon. This sort of job is not easy to get, but if you keep pestering – politely, of course – all the vets in your neighbourhood, you may get a Saturday or holiday hiring. You'll probably have to clean up, hold the cat or dog of some nervous elderly owner while your boss gives an injection, comfort pets coming out of anaesthesia after an operation, or accompany the vet on a trip to a local farm, perhaps, to help with a cow giving birth. It's smelly, messy work, that requires you to keep the highest standards of hygiene, but it's enthralling!

W1 WASHPERSON (*see also* LAUNDERETTE SERVICER)

Lots of busy families with their own washing-machines might pay for you to come in and see their wash and spin-drying through. Some have wardrobes of fashionable shirts and dresses needing hand-washing and very gentle pressing.

Keep a look-out among your neighbours for the clothes-conscious hurrying past in voile shirts, cheese-cloth tops or fine wool jerseys that would turn into rags in a machine. Take round anything of yours that needs careful washing and ironing as an example of your ability to do the work well. You can't expect to be paid as much as a professional launderer, but you could suggest a token low payment for the first pile and then, if they are satisfied, negotiate a reasonable fee.

W2 WATERING GARDENS

Some men love their smooth, emerald lawns more than their cars and yet they are often obliged to go away on holiday or business just when the dry season sets in. Automatic sprinklers are costly, and frequently go wrong.

Offer to water lawns for them daily. Be trustworthy and reliable. Don't drown the grass one evening because you're off for the weekend and not returning for three or four days. That's cheating. And the lawn will show you up, not to mention the neighbours.

W3 WINDOW-BOXING

Old people who are housebound or crippled, especially in city areas, love a flourishing, continually changing, flamboyant window-box. Offer to make or buy them one, fill it with plants, and restock it regularly. If you've got space, you can store the flowers past blooming time in your back garden for seeds or for use again next year. Make sure you have a written contract for the season if you are providing the box, earth and plants.

W4 WINDOW CLEANING

There are lots of householders who leave the cleaning to God, as they say, when it rains. But, usually in the spring or summer holidays, they notice that they can't see beyond the front gate.

This may sound a simple job that only requires lots of energy, bucket and cloths, and a head for heights, but *be careful*. Professional window cleaners on multi-storey flats have safety harnesses and hoists, by law.

So if it's beyond the ground floor, say that you will do as much as you can manage of the outsides or lower sills, without taking risks. This is important, because too many young window cleaners lose their balance and break a leg or worse. So, too bad if the householders complain that the top outside panes on the first floor haven't been done properly. Just tell them that it would be too dangerous for you, you've done your best, and they *will* just have to leave the rest to God and the rain!

To find your window cleaning, you could put a small advertisement in the local newsagent or go round neighbours. Have your own bucket and window-cleaning cloths – a small bottle of detergent and lots of absorbent rags, plus a chamois leather for the final rub, should be better and cheaper than most of the costly commercial window-cleaning products. Householders should be able to provide a small step-ladder if necessary and the water.

X1 EXTRA FOR FILMING

Do you happen to live near a film or TV studio? Do you know anybody who works in one?

Studios often need extras – people who stand in the crowd in the background or walk past in the film-set street, and who are not always professional actors. You don't necessarily need any acting ability. But you do need to be on the set on time, and possibly stand around for hours to be made-up and costumed and to wait for the stars to appear for the scene.

It doesn't matter if you think you aren't a bit good-looking: extras need to look like ordinary people – some fat, some skinny, some with interesting faces that were called ugly in their teens.

If you can, it is better to phone and ask what, if any, jobs are available (letters tend to get lost). Then ask when you can go for an interview. Sound keen, not over-modest. Show business is showing off as well as a lot of hard work. If you have taken the trouble to find out beforehand, from your newspaper or local gossip, what is being filmed, and ask to speak to the casting director in person, suggesting where you could fit in, that doubles your chances.

Y1 YACHT SCRUBBER

If your home is near a yacht marina, lake or the seaside, this is a much-welcomed chore for any boy or girl who doesn't mind scrubbing, swabbing down and polishing. Just go down to the harbour-master's office and ask for permission. He should take your name and address before letting you approach boat owners.

You may not be paid a lot, but if you have the decks immaculate and the brasswork gleaming, you could be invited on a swimming or fishing trip.

Y2 YOGA TRAINER

Perhaps you know some families with youngsters who

are always getting into trouble by behaving violently. Maybe it's because they live in a city, with not enough room and not enough to do. If you are a yoga fan, you could help them.

If you have read books on yoga (especially an excellent simple one for kids by Howard Kent), have been to classes, and enjoy it yourself, as a growing number of young people do, perhaps you could help others, and earn something towards your new ethnic cloak or organic food treats!

Offer to go round to the family home and give the kids a lesson for an hour a week. Show them how to be a lotus, a lapwing or a fir tree instead of driving Dad up the wall.

Z1 ZOO CLEANER

More and more cities, towns and holiday spots have a zoo or safari park. And, especially over weekends and during the holidays, they need extra help. This is probably a menial, dirty task, but if you are fascinated by animals, it could be a working paradise.

If you are trying for a job, ask one of the assistant keepers first what he or she thinks you should expect to be paid. Or ring up another zoo and ask them before your interview.

You will soon learn how important cleanliness is to avoid spreading disease, and there's nothing like a couple of weekends pushing a broom around or fetching the monkeys' supper to get you saving up for your own pets and thinking about whether or not you would like to become a zoo keeper.

4 KEEPING TO THE RULES

Not so long ago, little boys and girls were sent down mines, up chimneys and into factories to work for more than fourteen hours a day. This was unbelievably cruel.

Now there are laws governing the employment of young people, which are there to protect you. When you take your job, make sure that you know exactly what your local rules and regulations are. This is not easy! In Britain, they vary not only from one local authority to another, but even from one street to another.

In one district, you may have to ask the permission of the school secretary of your comprehensive before you can become a regular baby-sitter. In another, you can get away with it without mentioning it to anybody. Likewise, according to the law you can work for an uncle or aunt without having to keep to the time-work regulations on under-sixteens working, imposed by the Department of Health and Social Security or your local authority. One high-up civil servant told me: 'The laws on juvenile employment in Britain are a shambles.' So you have to work them out for yourself. Because, although there are laws protecting young people from working in factories, the by-laws (these are the rules decided by your local authority) are the ones that matter – the ones parents, teachers, employers and police have to abide by. And these can differ from street to street.

OK. So you don't wish to be an ill-paid slave. You don't want to take a half-wage out of the starved mouth of an unemployed man or woman who needs it for the kids or a home, when you are just saving up for a bike or a dress. But why shouldn't you have the chance to work at something nobody else wants? To help out for money, without doing anybody else out of a job, without breaking any laws?

Here are a few hints on how to keep to the rules. You'll find they are to your advantage.

First, you should ask your parents. Since it's probably quite a time since they were kids, they may not know the facts. Ask your teacher or tutor, the local neighbourhood advice centre and your local library. Ring up your local youth employment officer (see under the name of your local authority in the phone book for the number). Ask your local youth club manager and local sports club. Ask any young neighbours or friends who already have spare-time jobs.

You may discover that you are only allowed to work so many hours for so many days a week – or probably weekends only. A lot of sensible head teachers do not allow students who are working for exams to go on early-morning paper rounds, for instance, because they would be too tired to do schoolwork properly. But they do not mind you doing a Saturday morning job. You might be annoyed at missing the chance of extra money, but they are thinking of your future, and how much more you could earn by learning a bit more. You cannot fit too much into one day.

Does your Mum or Dad belong to a trade union? The Trades Union Congress offers guidelines on employment for under-sixteens, to schools. No harm in asking if you are a bit worried about conditions or wages. If you have applied for a job in your local supermarket as a cashier or a shelver, you might like to know that their union, USDAW, has a membership scheme for under-sixteens.

Lots of adults do not approve of child labour – not because they want you to do the washing up, but for more important reasons. They know from great-grandparents' tales what it was like for a bright boy or girl to have to help out by skivvying in Victorian times, leaving school as early as legally possible, losing the chance of a scholarship. Some had to slave at the factory bench until they dropped from hunger and exhaustion.

But you want to work, for fair recompense. So, having checked what the legal working hours are, I think you would be wise to write a letter of agreement. It could be along these lines:

Dear Mr Smith,

I am very pleased that you would like me to baby-sit/garden/help in shop for you regularly from next Monday, for a payment of £X per hour for four hours a week, Fridays and Saturdays.

I am prompt and reliable.

Yours sincerely,

Ann Jones

Get your employer to sign the letter and return it to you. Because you want to take a job, you probably like being independent, but it's not a bad idea to get your parents to sign the letter, too.

If you feel you are being underpaid or ill-treated in any way, ask any of the people mentioned above for their advice. One is bound to help you.

5 HOW TO BE A GOOD EMPLOYEE

Let's face it. There are bad employers and there are inefficient, lazy employees, too. Working for someone is a matter of square-dealing. You should expect fair payment for good work.

If this is your first time journeying out into the working world, you might like an idea of the rules your boss will ask you to keep – you'll find it helps you to do so.

Don't be Late

Are you good at getting up in the mornings, checking that you have got your watch on and the alarm is set, working out the bus or train times, to avoid queuing longer than you expected? If the answers are 'No', try harder. Sort it out. Because being there on the dot means a lot to your employer. Even if you don't feel very well – but not *really* ill – you should try to make it to the office, shop or house. Or at least phone or send a message well beforehand to say that you are not coming in. One of my helpmeets would ring to say she had a friend who would come instead (and I dropped everything for her wedding day).

Don't Truant

People who don't bother to turn up never keep jobs.

Don't Lie

You can't say Mum's ill every week when your boss

bumps into her on Saturdays in the supermarket, can you?

Don't Cheat or Steal

Is all the effort you put into stealing some goods from your place of work worth it? Are a boxful of knickers or shoes really worth what you could put into improving the business, bringing better rewards, pay or bonus?

Don't Make Promises You Can't Keep

If you say you'll do something, do it.

Give Reasonable Notice

If you are bored with your job or it is inconvenient, don't leave your employer in the lurch. Explain why you want to leave and, if you can, suggest somebody else who could take over from you. Then everybody's happy. Isn't there a boy or girl round the corner or up the stairs who would be grateful for a bit of extra cash? And you should ask your employer to give you references, too, which you can show to potential employers in the future.

Give a Bit Extra

You need not wait for a gravestone, to be appreciated! Wouldn't you like to be remembered – not to say recommended – for what you do?

Whatever job you take, wherever you're working, don't look upon your hours as sheer effort. Try to offer suggestions as to what fruit and veg should be offered on the market stall, what kind of books the baby might like for bedtime reading, how to sell dresses to customers without bullying them, or which cut of jeans sell best.

Accept Some Give and Take

Jobs like carpet-shampooing and baby-sitting may take longer than you expected or arranged for. But don't get angry if this happens and you get off later than agreed. Just suggest that you take time off next session or get some extra pay. If they are decent employers, they will probably offer first.

Smile!

There's nothing like one of those wide, wide, isn't-the-world-a-great-place beams for getting round tired mothers and tense bosses who are weary of moaners and whiners! And you're getting their money, too, aren't you?

6 HELPING YOUR MONEY GROW

What are you going to do with all this lovely lolly you've earned? Go on a spending spree that makes you happy on pay-day, a bit bereft, perhaps, the week after?

It's a lovely feeling to be able to march into the shop and pay for the camera, bike, fishing rod or dress you've been yearning for for weeks.

But maybe you've got long-term ideas, like saving up for something really costly or just putting the money away for a rainy day. So how will you hoard it? Keep it in a jam-jar on the kitchen shelf? This is asking for family trouble, because all but the wealthiest, most honourable mums and dads are bound to need to borrow something sooner or later. You'll find yourself landed with a lot of IOUs on the Saturday morning you want to buy a pair of sandals, and when you challenge them for repayment, they might feel so guilty about raiding your little bank that they'll take it out on you by losing their temper and telling you just how much you cost them in apple pies, trainers and tights.

Will you hoard it in a savings box on your bedroom shelf? Under the mattress? In your underwear drawer? Well, you know what happens to old people who do that with their life savings – these are the first places burglars look. And since you're working, you won't be sitting indoors all the time guarding your treasure, will you?

The best way is to deposit your money with a reliable financial institution that can offer you the best interest. Of course, you can hand it over to your parents for safe-keeping, for which they should give you a written agreement, but, if you are like most young people, you probably prefer to be independent and look after your money in your own way.

If you are putting your money into a commercial organization like an insurance company, this means that you deposit with them, say £100, and when they have used it to buy, sell or lend at a profit, they will give you a proportion of what they have gained from the use of it. So, at the end of a year, perhaps, you are entitled to withdraw £103. It's safe, it can't be stolen and you've gained £3. But you may not be able to withdraw the money before the year is out and some deposit agreements may be for several years.

Others are more flexible, and these are worth looking at. Maybe you are *not* one of those Saturday-morning spenders. Suppose, for instance, you have a cousin in Australia, who shares your ambition to set up a sports shop and training centre there. Your dream plan is to pay in, say, £12 a month from your spare-time earnings, while you go through university or college. By the time you have qualified, you could set sail or take flight with considerably more than your earnings in accrued interest – at least a third, according to some financial advisers. But there are schemes where – if you change your mind – you can cash in earlier than planned.

You can, of course, just put your money in a deposit box in your local bank. But then you would have to pay towards its safekeeping. The bank deposit box is really for people who want to stow away valuable jewels or legal documents.

What's your choice? In Britain, you've got quite a few. There's the Giro. Apply at your local Post Office for all the information and forms to fill in.

Then there's the School Bank. This is a bank backed by the National Savings Bank, but it is run by teachers and students. At least half the secondary schools in Britain have a school bank. You can put your money in and withdraw as much as you like whenever you like during the bank's opening times – usually during the dinner break or just after school. This, really, is for short-term savers only.

Or how about a building society? Well, sooner or later, you're going to want a home of your own. And if you've been paying into a society for, say, eight years regularly, this would make a great deal of difference to your chances of getting a mortgage.

One of the advantages of insurance companies is that, if you are a regular investor, they are a backing when you want to buy a house or start a business.

You could also open a savings account with a bank. Sooner or later, when you are earning full-time, you will probably want to open a current account, anyway. But it does no harm to take introductory leaflets from each and compare what they offer.

If you have parents, relatives, friends or teachers who are knowledgeable about saving, it is probably simpler to take their advice on what is the best way to store your money and watch it grow. But you can always annoy them by finding out for yourself, asking for leaflets from all these places, listing details and current interest rates, and comparing their advantages for yourself.

But don't forget to read the small type. It's no use handing over half your wages every week ready for your summer holiday, only to discover you cannot withdraw your money before Christmas.

If you are very bright at Maths and are the gambling type, you could take out some shares. Especially if you know some adults who could advise you on which is the sturdiest, most go-ahead company in which to invest your £30 or whatever. But this is a risk, since share values may fall if business is bad, and your £30 could end up as £15 or less. Just as it is not really satisfying to make a juicy profit out of other people with no effort on your part, it is even less pleasant to discover that half your hard-earned wages have disappeared into thin air.

You never know, maybe you'll end up giving your parents some advice on how to save their money!

Other titles in this series

KILL-A-LOUSE WEEK AND OTHER STORIES

Susan Gregory

The new head arrives at Davenport Secondary just at the beginning of the 'Kill-a-Louse' campaign. Soon the whole school is in uproar . . .

YATESY' RAP

Jon Blake

It was Ol's idea to play the Christmas concert. His second idea was to get a band together. A most unlikely band it turned out to be. Half of them couldn't play, most of them didn't like each other, and none of them had ever been on a stage. And then Yatesy arrived, with his reputation for being kicked out of several schools for fighting.

BREAKING GLASS

Brian Morse

When the Red Army drops its germ bomb on Leicester, the affected zone is sealed off permanently – with Darren and his sister Sally inside it. Immune to the disease which kills Sally, Darren must face alone the incomprehensible hatred of two of the few survivors trapped with him. And the haunting question is: why did Dad betray them?

AT THE SIGN OF THE DOG AND ROCKET

Jan Mark

When her father slips a disc, school-leaver Lilian Goodwin realizes she's in for a frantic couple of weeks in charge of the family's pub – and the last thing she needs is a rude and condescending temporary bar help like Tom to train.

BASKETBALL GAME

Julius Lester

Allen is black and Rebecca is white, and in Nashville, Tennessee, in 1956 that means they must keep apart. They're interested in eacy other, but is that enough to survive the deeply rooted prejudice that surrounds them?

LOCKED IN TIME

Lois Duncan

When seventeen-year-old Nore arrives at the old Louisiana plantation home of her father and his new wife, she is prepared for unhappiness. She did not expect her new family to be so different, nor can she understand her own mixed-up feelings about them. Her new mother is exotically beautiful, yet Nore senses evil . . .